America's Fighting Railroads

A World War II Pictorial History

"With confidence in our Armed Forces,
With the unbounding determination of our people,
We will gain the inevitable triumph,
So help us God!"

FRANKLIN D. ROOSEVELT
December 8, 1941

What We Fight For

Efficiency FOR VICTORY

Our nation being at war again, on this 166th anniversary of the Declaration of Independence, today is a good time to consider what our ancestors fought for, and for what we are fighting.

They fought for *freedom*. "Democracy," for which many say we are fighting, is not mentioned in the Declaration, the Constitution or the national anthems "Star Spangled Banner" and "America." Among men's "unalienable rights" the Declaration names "life, *liberty* and the pursuit of happiness." The Constitution sets forth that it is adopted by "We the people," to "secure the blessings of *liberty* to ourselves and our posterity." To this end "The United States shall guarantee to every state . . . a *republican*" (i.e., a *representative*, not a "democratic") "form of government."

The Constitution requires *freedom* of religion, of speech, and of the press, and provides that no person shall "be deprived of life, liberty or *property* without due process of law; nor shall *private property* be taken for public use without just compensation."

Note that the repeated emphasis is on *liberty, freedom;* that in the Constitution life, liberty and *property* are all assured protection (from government) in *one sentence;* and that in that same sentence *private property* is guaranteed full protection.

The personal freedom and private property guaranteed provide for *free private enterprise*. And free private enterprise is the *necessary* foundation of all the other freedoms. For only under free private enterprise can men make their livings as they please; and to maintain effective dictation of how they shall make their livings government must deprive them of all freedom, by word or act, to oppose its policies.

What our ancestors declared for 166 years ago, and fought for and established, then, was a system of *political* liberty and *free private enterprise*. And that, if we are fighting for the only thing that makes living worth while, is what we are fighting for now.

Our railroads are one of our finest examples of free private enterprise. What they have achieved for the nation during the last two years, and are still achieving, in efficiency and economy, never has been, never could be, equalled in peace or war by any dictatorial government bureaucracy. For it is the result of thousands of widely-scattered *free* men exercising their full initiative and energy in *free* co-operation—which government bureaucracy, by its nature, prevents.

Said the House Committee on Military Affairs in a recent report: "Unbelievable red tape, top-heavy organization and lack of orientation to a state of war still lead the parade in war-time Washington . . . Nearly every conceivable type of extravagant waste has been reflected by these investigations." Nothing of that kind has been, or could be, said about our private-enterprise operation of railroads during the same period.

We will, if we know what we are doing, both "for the duration" and afterward, fight for *freedom* as meant by the Declaration and the Constitution—*freedom from domination of person or property by any government*, foreign or domestic—and fight as hard for it at home as abroad.

America's Fighting Railroads

A World War II Pictorial History

BY DON DeNevi

LIBRARY OF CONGRESS CATALOG CARD NO. 96-68879

ISBN 1-57510-001-0

First Printing: May 1996
Second Printing: March 1997
Third Printing: November 1998
Fourth Printing: October 2000

Typography: Arrow Graphics, Missoula, Montana.
Layout: Stan Cohen, Missoula, Montana.

ON THE COVER:

These troops were some of the lucky ones, traveling on Pullman cars. A few of the 202 men who were sent
to McDill Field, Tampa, Fla.; Camp Sereven, Camp Stewart and Charleston, S.C., pose for this
flash photo at Fort McPherson, Atlanta, Ga. USASC

PICTORIAL HISTORIES PUBLISHING COMPANY
713 South Third Street West, Missoula, Montana 59801

INTRODUCTION

THE WAR IN WHICH the United States found itself in December of 1941 made greater demands upon transportation than any conflict in its history. This fact was spectacularly illustrated by the vast distances that American troops and supplies had to traverse to reach such faraway stations and combat areas as Australia, the Solomon Islands, and North Africa. At the time, the railroads had so much less equipment than a decade before that it seemed improbable they would be able to meet all the demands for both freight and passenger service, which far exceeded expectations. But, by the end of World War II, the nation's railroads had doubled the freight traffic and quadrupled the passenger traffic handled by them. In mid-1945, they had succeeded in virtually remedying all the major problems during the four years of war effort, including severe winters, car-loadings, minimum transports, etc. And, never since Pearl Harbor had the greatest war effort for production and combat ever made by any nation been hampered by lack of railroad service.

What follows is a graphic appreciation of patriotic and effective endeavor by railroad management, railroad employees, and shippers and government agencies that have cooperated with those railroads. In these magnificently illustrated pages, whose pictures were taken by some of America's leading railroad and military photographers, the reader will find various types of locomotives, most in action, hauling military movements, wartime freight, and passenger trains turned troop carriers. This illustrated memoir should prove of the greatest interest to World War II buffs, railroad fans, model builders, photographers, hobbyists, and Canadian and American citizens.

ABOUT THE AUTHOR

In addition to teaching courses in psychology at the College of Alameda, in Alameda, California, and to inmates serving life sentences at Soledad State Prison, near Salinas, California, DeNevi has authored 28 books, including *Riddle of the Rock—The Only Successful Escape from Alcatraz*. His other volumes range in subjects from California history to space flight, earthquake science, World War II railroad mobilization, and biographies.

DeNevi graduated in 1959 from the University of the Pacific in Stockton, California, with a B.A. in history and art. He subsequently earned his Masters and Ed.D. in Education from the University of California at Berkeley. He has been affiliated with college teaching for the past 35 years. In addition to his writing (he has several movie treatments in circulation), he paints watercolors of imaginary, whimsical cities, birds, butterflies, and landscapes.

PHOTO SOURCES

AAR—Association of American Railroads
AMHA—Anchorage Museum of History & Art
ATSF—Atchison, Topeka & Santa Fe Railway
B&M RR—Boston & Maine Railroad
B&O RR—Baltimore & Ohio Railroad
CBQRR—Chicago, Burlington & Quincy Railroad
DRGWRR—Denver & Rio Grande Western Railroad
GMC—General Motors Corporation
ICRR—Illinois Central Railroad
LC—Library of Congress
L&N—Louisville & Nashville Railroad

NA—National Archives
NYCRR—New York Central Railroad
NW—Norfolk & Western Railroad
PRR—Pennsylvania Railroad
RNE—Railway Negative Exchange
RPS—Rail Photo Service
SPRR—Southern Pacific Railroad
UPRR—Union Pacific Railroad
USASC—U.S. Army Signal Corps
USN—U.S. Navy
YA—Yukon Archives

ACKNOWLEDGMENTS

This illustrated memoir required help when it began to be assembled in 1976, and that help was given generously by many individuals. These people, many of them good friends, were of invaluable assistance, especially in terms of identifying photographs. Probably the most significant help came from Warren Miller, who owned the nationally known and respected Railway Negative Exchange in Moraga, Calif.; J. Ronald Shumate, Media Specialist of the Association of American Railroads; John C. McLeod, Librarian, Economics and Finance Department, Association of American Railroads; Donna J. Voight of the U.S. Army Still Photo Library in the Pentagon; John E. Witherbee, Public Relations Officer of the Union Pacific Railroad; John Nagle, Public Relations Director of the Burlington-Northern Railroad; and Robert Sullivan, Public Relations Officer of the Santa Fe Railroad. All of these fine people answered questions, verified inquiries, and provided rare photographs. Without their help the book would not have been completed.

Also, the author is indebted to hundreds of magazine articles and books that focused on the role of America's railroads during World War II. It would be a crime not to acknowledge the most important. These sources provided the information for the book. Perhaps the serious reader will want to further research the following authors and titles: S. Kip Farrington, Jr., *Railroads At War* (Coward-McCann; New York, 1944); John F. Stover, *The Life and Decline of the American Railroad* (Oxford University Press; New York, 1970); James Marshall, *Santa Fe: The Railroad That Built An Empire* (Random House; New York, 1945); Gen. James A. Van Fleet, *Rail Transport and the Winning of Wars* (Association of American Railroads; Washington, D.C., 1956); Carl R. Gray, Jr., *Railroading in Eighteen Countries* (Charles Scribner's Sons; New York, 1955); and Edward Hungerford, *Transport for War, 1942–1943* (E.P. Dutton; New York, 1943).

Although the author browsed through hundreds of articles, the most important were *Life* magazine's "Railroads at War" (Sept. 21, 1942); *Railway Age's* "1942 Railway Operations Reviewed" (Jan. 3, 1943), and *Fortune Magazine's* "All Out from the Neck Up" (July 1942); "How Much in the Railroads?" (January 1945); "The Working Front: Rock Island Revisited" (January 1945); "The Working Front: They're Crowding the Rails" (November 1942); "How the Railroads Did It" (November 1942); and "The Westward Empire" (July 1942).

For

WARREN MILLER

1923–1989

who singularly brought new life to the historic railroad photograph

This book would not have been possible without the rich and varied photographic collection of the Railway Negative Exchange, founded and maintained by Warren Miller. In fact, it evolved out of my long-standing friendship with Warren, whose generous guidance and donation of certain carefully selected photographs leaves me in debt I cannot repay. Born in Oakland, California, Warren was this nation's foremost authority on the western railroad and devoted virtually his entire life to assembling more than a quarter of a million negatives, most in glass plates, as well as some 200,000 photographs. Warren understood I did not intend an exhaustive and scholarly account of one of America's greatest mobilization efforts. Yet, he felt so strongly about telling the story, no matter how introductory, that he offered his choicest photos.

Today, that collection is maintained by Warren's nephew, Bob Hall. Bob and I co-authored *The United States Military Railway Service—America's Soldier-Railroaders in World War II* (Boston Mills Press, 1990), an account of our country's efforts to keep the war-torn railroads of Europe running during World War II. Almost all the historic photos in that text were selected from the Railway Negative Exchange. For further information about the Exchange, or to contact Bob, write The Railway Negative Exchange, 1496 Los Rios Drive, San Jose, CA 95120.

DON DENEVI

TABLE OF CONTENTS

Introduction   v

Acknowledgments   vi

I. THE BIGGEST JOB IN RAILROAD HISTORY   1

II. THE FIGHT FOR FREEDOM   25
Organization For War
America's Railway Service in 1941–1942
Massing For Total War
The Role Of Southern Pacific in 1942
1942: The Year All Railroad Records Were Broken

III. THE MILITARY RAILWAY SERVICE   51
The Alaska Railroad During World War II
The Alaskan White Pass and Yukon Route

IV. 1943-1944: VICTORIES ON ALL FRONTS   73
1944 Railway Operations
The Diesel-Electric Locomotive: Making Railroad Utilization More Known
The Military Railway Service Drives Toward Berlin

V. FINAL VICTORY: GREAT DAYS AHEAD FOR AMERICA'S RAILROADS
A JOB STILL TO BE FINISHED   99

VI. CONCLUSION   107
Plans For the Postwar Traveler

VII. POST SCRIPT—OTHER MEANS OF TRANSPORTATION
USED IN THE WAR EFFORT   109

VIII. PHOTOGRAPHS, CHARTS, WARTIME ADS   119

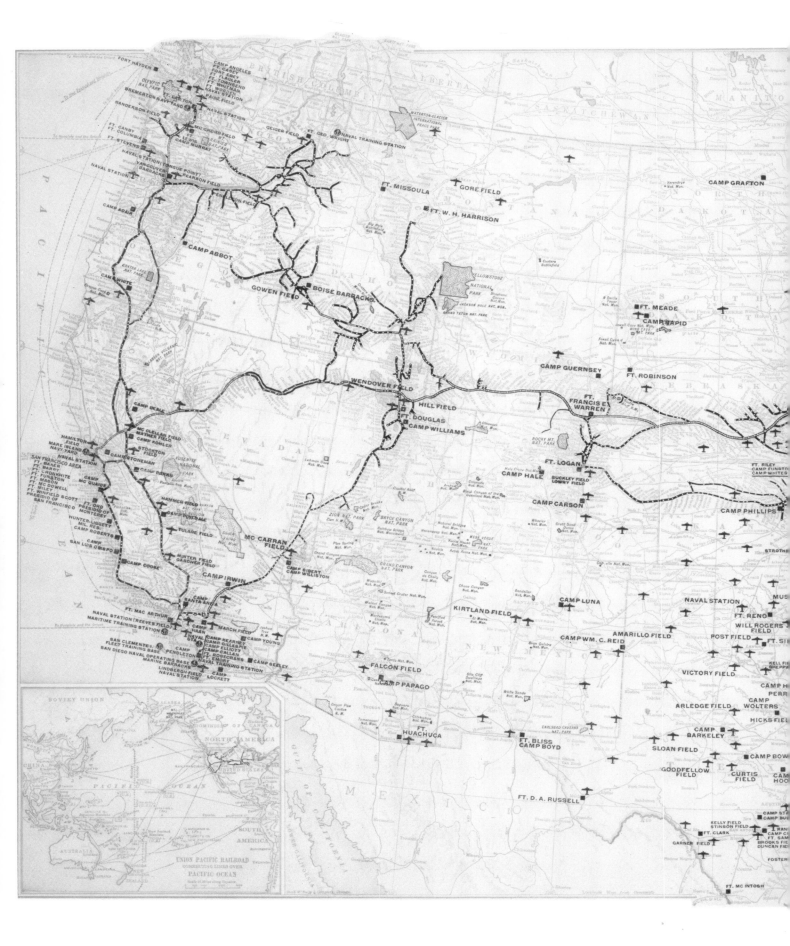

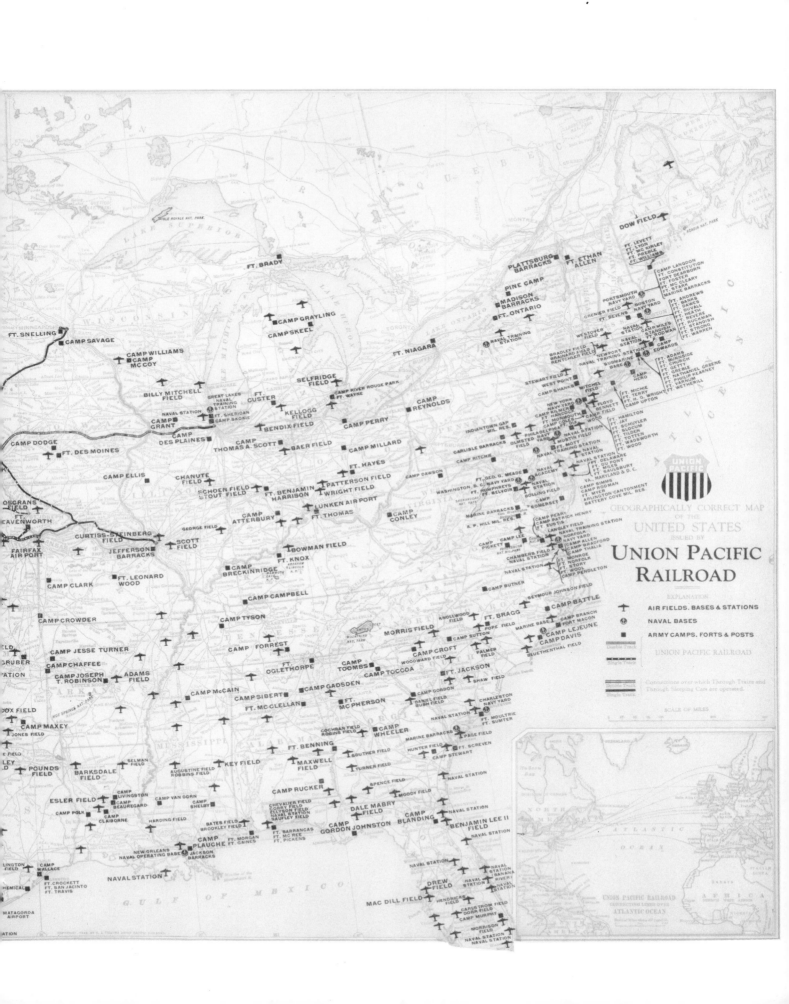

GEOGRAPHICALLY CORRECT MAP
OF THE
UNITED STATES
ISSUED BY

UNION PACIFIC RAILROAD

EXPLANATION

✈ AIR FIELDS, BASES & STATIONS
⚓ NAVAL BASES
■ ARMY CAMPS, FORTS & POSTS

UNION PACIFIC RAILROAD

Connections over which Through Trains and
Through Sleeping Cars are operated.

SCALE OF MILES

UNION PACIFIC RAILROAD
CONNECTING LINES OVER THE
ATLANTIC OCEAN

These troops were some of the lucky ones, traveling on Pullman cars. A few of the 202 men who were sent to McDill Field, Tampa, Florida; Camp Sereven, Camp Stewart and Charleston, S.C., pose for this flash photo at Fort McPherson, Atlanta, Ga. USASC

1

. . . .

The Biggest Job in Railroad History

"I've seen a locomotive over 130 feet long, speeding war material over mountain grades. I've watched troops unloading from train after train, powered by fast Diesel or Steamliners, some with 7,000 horsepower, the heaviest and most powerful ever made. And, I never witnessed a speed-up so swift, or so well directed, as men and women of America's railroads swarmed to their tasks of building even more powerful locomotives, laying more tracks, and organizing incredibly complex shipping schedules. We Americans needed a miracle in railroad transportation during early 1942, we expected that miracle, and, by George, we got that miracle!

LOWELL THOMAS IN A NEWS SUMMARY,
May 12, 1942

No history of America's railroads can ever be complete unless a chapter is devoted to the job each one of those railroads did during World War II. At a time when congestion and car shortage meant possible disaster for mankind halfway around the globe, the railroads of the United States completed the biggest transportation job in the history of the world. In fact, the railroads were termed the first American task force, since they had the job of assembling huge quantities of men and materials for the first battles—Guadalcanal, Tunisia, Attu, and Sicily.

Late on the afternoon of Dec. 7, 1941, the War Department flashed orders to training camps. Almost overnight, trains were loaded throughout the land with troops and equipment destined for ports of embarkation or coastal defenses. Within a span of a few weeks, more troops were moved than during the first eight months of World War I. And, of course, this was only a starter. Soon, trainloads of ship steel were rushed to the Pacific Coast to repair the Pearl Harbor damage.

Materials for building new shipyards and for the ships themselves were gathered from all over the country by the railroads. Huge new airplane, tank, and munitions factories blossomed everywhere.

Construction material and machinery flowed in an ever-increasing tide over the country's steel rails. Meanwhile, there was an immediate need for new army camps and airfields. In spite of the fact that America's railroad companies had 32 percent fewer locomotives than in World War I, railborne freight tonnage zoomed—and this only because the power of the average locomotive had been increased more than 50 percent and the speed of freight trains increased more than 30 percent in those intervening years. With submarine warfare closing many of the water routes through the Panama Canal, and Atlantic coastwise shipping virtually coming to a standstill during the first year after the outbreak of hostilities, America turned to the railroads in the emergency. As the vast tonnage shifted from water and highway to the rails, the loads doubled,

And the big guns rode the rails. This mid-1930 shot of Sacramento, Calif., shows one of the West Coast's Mobile/Rail Coast Defense Guns. These guns were salvaged from large naval vessels after World War I and modified for use as coast defense guns—both mobile and stationary. The largest rigid steam engines on the SP were assigned the task of hauling these heavy loads over the tracks of the Southern Pacific—usually at night. Engine #5003, 4-12-2, was assigned to the gun train at the time this photo was snapped. Very little is known about the operations of these mobile guns up and down the coast, either before or during World War II. RNE

A panoramic view of the "Big Gun" also shows some heavy-duty railroad equipment on flat car in foreground. This complicated piece of equipment apparently was used by the Southern Pacific Railroad in maintenance. RNE

. . .

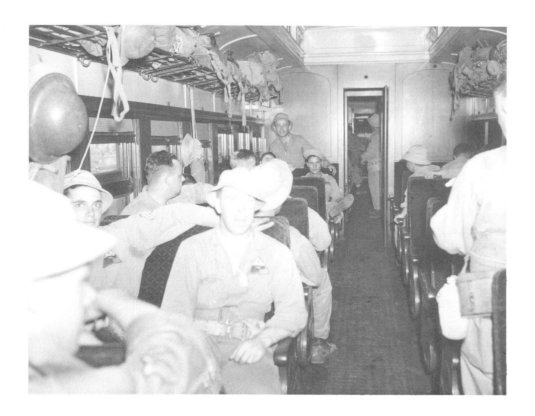

Soldiers of the 1st Armored Division ride on their way to Louisiana maneuvers from Fort Knox in a Day Clean Day Coach, September 1941. Note the World War I helmet, which clarifies that this was taken before the war. AAR

GIs in fatigues on the move. Soldiers on the 1st Armored Division boarding their train at Ft. Knox, heading for field maneuvers in Louisiana in September 1941. USASC

Nighttime, somewhere in California, troops waiting for SP's 3767, as a second section of Train 20 is on its northward run to Portland. This August 1940 photograph shows the California State National Guard troops on their way to maneuvers at Ft. Lewis, Wash. SPRR

Automobile cars carried Army vehicles to 3rd Army Maneuvers at Fort Benning, Ga., in April 1940. This photo shows how vehicles were carried inside the large automobile cars. This equipment belonged to the 3rd Army in those days before the war. USASC

The big guns move by rail. Here we see a 155mm gun at the Fort Benning railhead during the 3rd Army Maneuvers in April 1940. USASC

This October 1941 view shows horses about to be loaded onto the stock cars at the left for movement from Rosslyn, Va., to Chester, S.C., for maneuvers. Horses were quickly replaced by motor vehicles at the start of the war. The railroads were ready for the change-over and handled thousands of train loads of heavy armor throughout the war years. USASC

Duty in the pre-war days. Troopers of the 92nd Reconnaissance Squadron 2nd Cavalry Div., Camp Funston, Kansas, sleeping between shifts of night guard duty. They were guarding a shipment of gold, which was awaiting transfer to the Denver Mint. Nov. 21, 1941, just a few days before Pearl Harbor. US ARMY 162ND SIGNAL PHOTOGRAPHIC CO.

The 92nd Reconnaissance Squadron guarding a gold shipment at Union Station, Denver, Colo., on Nov. 18, 1941. This shipment from the West Coast arrived in Denver on a Southern Pacific Railway post office car, and then was transferred to U.S. Mail trucks. Note that three of the mail trucks have armored driver's cabs. US ARMY 162ND SIGNAL PHOTOGRAPHIC CO.

And the big ones went by rail. This 68-foot coast defense gun, snapped in the San Francisco Bay area, was transported by rail across the country from Massachusetts to California on this special flat car. The two civilian workers are preparing the gun for unloading in a railroad yard, possibly on the Northwestern Pacific Railroad at Sausalito — the nearest railhead to Fort Barry & Fort Cronkite, which guarded San Francisco Bay with its hidden coast defense guns on the north side of the Golden Gate Straits. The NWP RR is owned by the Southern Pacific Railroad. SPRR

More guns on the move. Here we have a shipment of naval guns awaiting arrival of a steam engine. Note that two flat cars were used for each gun, and they were secured differently from the photo taken of the Army Coast defense gun. This view taken in the Navy Yard, Washington, D.C. Catenary indicates that rail line to the right is that of the Pennsylvania Railroad. USN

Pre-war maneuvers . . . and the railroads were there. Half/tracks of the 1st Armored Division being transferred by rail from Ft. Knox to Louisiana troop maneuvers in September 1941. ARR

. . .

7

then doubled again.

With the railroads being called upon to move the greatest volume of freight in history, everyone knew the job would require every possible spark of ingenuity, ability, and efficiency of railroad management and men. Above all, it would be a job that demanded the utmost cooperation among the railroads, shippers and receivers, and government, completely utilizing every railroad facility. Because the railroads would be allowed only a moderate number of new cars and locomotives, every railroad car would have to be loaded quickly, carry a capacity load, be properly consigned and carefully handled, be moved swiftly to its destination, and unloaded promptly and released immediately. In short, every foot of car space would have to be used and every minute utilized to its fullest. Personnel from the armed forces as well as railroad management and employees realized that these commonsense practices were vital to the war effort. The cry of the nation's railroaders was "Load 'em and unload 'em, while we'll move 'em." And they did.

Although a tremendous burden was thrust upon the railroads during the afternoon of Dec. 7, 1941, they were in a far better position to carry it than they had been in 1917, when the United States declared war on the Kaiser of Germany. In December of 1941, America had at her disposal more than 41,000 locomotives, 2,000,000 freight cars, and 230,000 miles of rail lines. And these figures represent fewer engines, fewer cars, and fewer miles of track than what had been available in 1917; two-thirds as many cars as 1920 and almost half as many locomotives. Yet by August of 1942, American railroads had carried over 600,000,000-ton-miles of freight. In the first seven months of that year, nearly 2,000,000 troops were moved every month.

No one in America appreciated such figures more than President Franklin D. Roosevelt, a man who had always been considered a friend of the railroads. In his thirteen years in the White House, the President traveled over 250,000 miles by railroad. During World War I, Roosevelt, as Secretary of the Navy, had understood the need for government operations of the railroads. As World War II approached, and America's participation an obvious possibility, the President asked to be briefed on the improvements in operating efficiency that had been made by the nation's railroad companies.

Ralph Budd, an old-time friend of Roosevelt and President of the Burlington Railroad, was an early promoter of diesel-engine streamlined passenger trains. In late September of 1939, he was summoned to the White House for a conference. Before Roosevelt could greet his friend, so the story goes, Budd urged Roosevelt to leave the railroads under private direction. The President laughed and said he had no intention whatsoever to take over the railroads as Wilson had done in 1917. Relieved, Budd recommended that a fully coordinated wartime transport service be established by coordination with such agencies as the Shippers' Advisory Boards, the Interstate Commerce Commission, and the Association of American Railroads. Roosevelt agreed with the concept.

Congressional leaders look on as President Roosevelt signs the bill that declared the United States as being in a state of war with the Japanese Empire. Dec. 8, 1941. USASC

Four days after Pearl Harbor, Ralph Budd, transportation commissioner, writes to General Somervell.

December 11, 1914

Brigadier General Brehon B. Somervell
War Department
2149 Munitions Building
Washington, D.C.

Dear General Somervell:

I did not trouble you with telephone advice about troop movements from Fort Bliss and Camp Hulen, which you mentioned yesterday evening, because I understood you were getting further advice about it, but I want you to have a copy of the report which I got for you on these movements, as follows:

"With regard to Fort Bliss, we received information on this from the Quartermaster General for the first time at 6:45 p.m. on December 8. This information did not have anything except the bare fact that certain Coast Artillery Units would move from that station as quickly as possible for the West and that we would later be given details as to numbers of trains, destinations, etc. We immediately sent out a warning to the originating carriers, our telegram being filed at 6:55 p.m. on December 8. Trains began moving out of Fort Bliss at 2:30 p.m. December 9. The second train departed 6:05 pm. December 9; the third train 8:05 pm. December 9; the fourth train 12:05 a.m. December 10; the fifth train 5:39 a.m. December 10; the sixth train 2:50 p.m. December 10; the seventh train 5:45 p.m. December 10; these all moved via the Southern Pacific. The eighth train moved via the Santa Fe and departed 7:15 a.m. December 10 and passed El Paso 9:12 a.m. December 10; the ninth train departed 1:05 p.m. from the Camp and passed El Paso at 10:45 p.m. December 10. Train No. 11 departed 5:47 a.m. December 11. This train was loaded in the Santa Fe Yards and as of 9:00 a.m. this morning, Central Time, two more trains were in the process of loading. This leaves five yet to go from Bliss and as of 9 a.m. this morning the necessary equipment was in place.

"In connection with this movement I would like to point out that the first train moved out of Fort Bliss in 19 hours, 35 minutes from the time we gave the railroads the first flash of this prospective movement. With such short time to get equipment into place and ready for loading, you will understand some of the things that had to be done: drop-end gondolas were not available in the quantity necessary and the railroad put on bridge crews who sawed the ends out of low side gondolas in order to make an open end gon; the facilities at Fort Bliss are very limited and it was not possible to load up more than one unit at a time, therefore, the 63rd was held up until the 260th was out of the way.

"At Camp Hulen, another point at which we had some difficulty, we got the first flash on this at 8:05 p.m. December 8 and the first train moved at 2:45 p.m. December 9; the second train at 6:20 p.m. December 9; the third train at 10:40 p.m. December 9; the fourth train at 2:10 a.m. December 10; the fifth train at 4 a.m. December 10; the sixth train at 11 a.m. December 10; the seventh train at 2:10 p.m. December 10; the eighth train at 3:45 p.m. December 10; the ninth train at 6:20 p.m. December 10; the tenth train at 7:00 p.m. December 10; the eleventh train at 10:45 p.m. December 10; the twelfth train at 6:00 a.m. December 11.

"At Camp Hulen exceedingly heavy rains and deep mud somewhat hampered operations. Another difficulty was the inexperienced loading crews, and, in an endeavor to assist loading operations, Southern Pacific put in a 21-man crew, bridge men, to assist in blocking, bracing and wiring the material—this will effect a little faster movement because we have run into difficulty on the same material loaded by Army personnel by having to stop trains en route for restacking and rewiring cars. Another difficulty is the fact that the Procurement Officer at Camp Hulen had no money to buy material for the necessary blocking and bracing; this also slowed up operations.

"In addition to the loading at Camp Hulen proper, it was found that the conditions surrounding the loading so congested facilities that one regiment of 197 going to New York was brought out of Hulen overland to Houston and loaded at that point in the Eureka Yards. The first train on this move departed Houston at 10:35 p.m. December 10 and was followed by four additional trains, departing at 4 a.m., 6:55 a.m., 8:20 a.m. and 10:30 a.m. today." [from A.H. Gass, Dec/11/41]

The movements from these points and from several other points, some details of which have come to my attention, lead me to say that I believe all of the Railway Operating people appreciate the vital importance of giving military transportation first and preferred attention. They are usually quite resourceful and I believe that they can be relied upon for full cooperation. I find that the twenty-five mile an hour schedule which you mentioned yesterday was discontinued some time ago, and that trains are being moved with speed consistent with safety operation.

Yours sincerely,
(SGD) RALPH BUDD
Transportation Commissioner.

Soldiers stationed at the Boston Army Base, Boston, Mass., listening to President Roosevelt's speech on the Declaration of War, Dec. 8, 1941. USASC

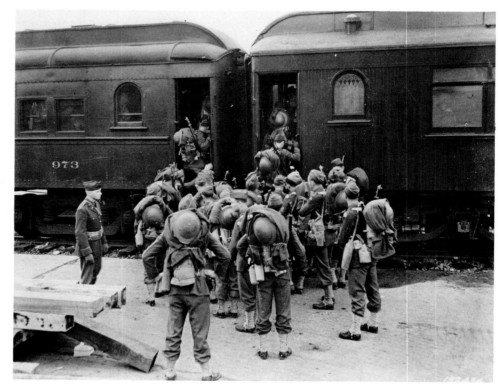

World War I helmets on their backs, garrison caps on their heads, these pre-war GIs wait their turn to enter obsolete passenger cars. Note the car on the right is of wooden construction. This is part of the 35th Division boarding in preparation for leaving Camp Robinson, Ark., on Dec. 18, 1941, 11 days after Pearl Harbor. USASC

. . .

*I*n early May of 1940, the President went before Congress to ask for a huge increase in defense expenditures. In early June, Roosevelt created a Council of National Defense, as well as an Advisory Commission to the Council consisting of seven transportation experts. Budd was appointed by the President (and Congress agreed) to serve as the Commissioner of Transportation. His chief responsibility would be to coordinate all truck, bus, air, pipeline, and railroad activity in America. After Budd arrived in Washington, D.C., and established his office, he decided that his first objective would be to appraise as realistically as possible the nation's transportation needs during the coming years. According to historian John F. Stover in his fine book, *The Life and Decline of the American Railroad* (1970), "The range of Budd's duties was wide. He urged the construction of new access highways to improve truck transport, he helped set up additional ice-breaking services, which allowed the 1941 Great Lakes navigation season to be of record length, and he so motivated his fellow rail executives that by November 1941 the bad-order freight car ratio (the percentage of freight cars out of service for repair work) was at an all-time low. Though Budd had few mandatory powers, he had managed, through a combination of consultation and broad cooperation, to avoid many of the problems that bothered the transportation systems that had served during World War I."

A few days after Pearl Harbor, President Roosevelt, under his emergency powers, established the Office of Defense Transportation, with Joseph B. Eastman as director. As a former member of the I.C.C. and Federal Coordinator of Transportation between 1933 and 1936, Joe was charged with conserving equipment (through such methods as heavier loading of freight cars), the reduction of circuitous routing, limitation of diversions and reconsignments, the prompt loading and unloading of freight, the diversion of traffic from routes that were becoming congested, and the scheduling of petroleum products in solid trains of tank cars to the Eastern Seaboard territory. The Interstate Commerce Commission, as well as various state regulatory bodies, was ordered to cooperate with the new Office of Defense Transportation.

Of course, Eastman depended a great deal on the foundation Budd built. However, the new Office of Defense Transportation did not get all it wanted in terms of railroad equipment and supplies since the ever-watchful War Production Board was in a trimming mood during that year of war. The O.D.T. was allowed only 38 percent of the 300,000 new freight cars Eastman requested and only 62 percent of the 4,200 locomotives requested. But Eastman, like Budd, was determined to escape Federal operation of the transportation system during the national emergency through preparedness and marked efficiency of his railroads.

According to John Stover, "One of Eastman's most pressing problems was the substantial decline in equipment and personnel which had developed in the years since World War I. As compared with 1917, the rail industry in 1942 had 32% fewer locomotives, 24% fewer freight cars, and 35% fewer passenger cars. The number of railroad workers had declined nearly 27% in the same twenty-five years. But the smaller roster of employees in 1942 was running heavier engines which produced a greater average tractive effort permitting longer, heavier, and faster trains. The capacity of the average freight car had been increased so greatly in the quarter of a century, from forty-one to fifty tons, that the 1,745,000 freight cars in 1942 had an aggregate capacity not noticeably less than all the cars carrying the war traffic of 1917. And the 42,000 locomotives which moved World War II troops and war material had a total tractive effort roughly as great as the more numerous steamers of the 'teens.'"

During those first months of World War II, said an official at Sante Fe, the "sinews of war surged unceasingly from the mountains, the plains, the seashore, all along the vast network of railroads that for the past 100 years had been building this great country of ours" and, of course, he was right. Between the first World War and Pearl Harbor, the railways had been modernizing. Billions of dollars were spent to improve tracks, roadways, and signals, as well as to build better equipment and improve transportation techniques. Critics insisted that these were wasted dollars since America's railroads were inefficient, old-fashioned, and over-built. The advocates of other forms of transportation felt the railroads should be relegated to the horse-and-buggy status. But, by Dec. 15, 1941, the critics were proven wrong. Week after week, war emergency needs established new railroad performance records. Even in the face of material shortages when new cars and new locomotives were not to be had for replacing worn equipment, railroad men found ingenious ways to get their jobs done. Trains continued to haul as repairs were made from salvaged pieces as well as substitute materials. Meanwhile, the critics were right when they predicted that millions of men in uniforms, thousands of miles from home, would create a transportation problem unique in the country's history. During World War I, soldiers averaged two trips by rail before embarkation. Authorities predicted that in the coming months and years of World War II soldiers would average six rail trips with the mileage of each trip increased in proportion. Soldiers, sailors, and marines, singly and in groups, in carloads and trainloads became daily events on most railroads. In fact, during the first two years of war, 65 percent of all the Pullman cars and many railroad-owned coaches were under constant military orders.

To handle such troop movements, Uncle Sam incorporated Centralized Traffic Control, a system providing a single-track line with 75 percent of double-track capacity. Actually, C.T.C. had been initiated in late 1927. In a nutshell, C.T.C. placed complete control of switches and signals over extended distances of track at the tips of a train dispatcher's fingers. It eliminated train orders and time lost by trains "in the hole," and had proven a vital cog in many of the nation's strategic rail lines. According to S. Kip Farrington Jr., in his book *Railroads at War* (1944), figures from the Interstate Commerce Commission show that by the end of 1929 there were twenty-six installations in service. During the following three years, the figure tripled.

By the end of 1935, there were 160 installations. Centralized Traffic Control systems installed in 1942 and 1943 alone totalled 1,600 miles, or over 60 percent of all mileage completed before 1942.

Because of men like Budd and Eastman, and innovative administrative departments such as Centralized Traffic Control and Office of Defense Transportation, the trains of America went through with their passengers, materials, mail, and express. And, the schedules were maintained remarkably well.

Rear Admiral William Brent Young, U.S.N., said in June of 1942, "The efficiency and dispatch of our railroads in moving millions of tons of freight for the Armed Forces, and in transporting hundreds of thousands of men from their homes to training stations and from stations to ports, have already established records during the first six months of war unparalleled in the history of transportation. The records which have been achieved by the railroads, with less rolling stock and fewer locomotives than were available during the first World War, must be recognized as among the greatest American accomplishments in the prosecution of the war."

Empire State Express on the move. The Empire State Express was one of the key trains operated by the NYC out of New York City in the war years. NYCRR

Juice jack on the New Haven Road. Typical pre-war passenger local on the NYNH&H RR, trains like this ran all through the war years. H.W. PONTIN PHOTO

City of San Francisco along the Truckee River. This pre-war photo is a good example of what this world-famous Oakland to Chicago streamliner looked like out on the line. The City of San Francisco ran all through the war years with an excellent record, though most of us rode the slower "Overland Limited" and other lesser-known trains, we always had hopes of ridin' the "City" and envied those who did.
SP PHOTO COURTESY OF RNE

The Black Diamond-Illinois Central Railroad's pre-war streamliner. It was the railroad's gamble to invest in streamlined trains such as the Black Diamond during the depression years of the mid-1930s that gave them a head start when the war came in December 1941. These diesel/electric stream-lined passenger trains were run well beyond what they were built for during the war. You will note that the first car of this train was a Railway Post Office, giving this train two purposes: to move people at the fastest possible speed and to carry the mail, which was sorted by postal clerks as the train sped on to its destination. ICRR

· · ·

13

Steam freight through Jackson, Miss. Date of this photo is unknown, but it does show the heavyweight type of coaches that hauled troops on short hauls during World War II. This Illinois Central freight pulled by No. 1493 has just cleared the station area and starts speeding up for its run down the main line. C.W. WITBECK PHOTO VIA ARR

Pennsylvania 4354. This heavy 2-8-0 with a long train of empties on its way back to the coal mines struggles up the world-famous Horseshoe Curve. The Pennsylvania RR being in the middle of the Pennsylvania coal region carried a large amount of coal to the war industries. RPS

. . .

Harpers Ferry, W.Va., is the location of this shot of a Baltimore & Ohio Railroad combination Coal & Tank Car train crossing the Potomac River. The B&O, whose track more or less served the same area as the Pennsylvania Railroad also had its share of wartime fuel trains. This shot shows the steamer on the bridge with fully loaded train. Harpers Ferry Station can be seen across the river where the train takes the curve. B&O RR

Pre-war Streamliner. This streamlined passenger train of the NYC Railroad takes a curve at high speed in the days prior to Pearl Harbor. The NYC Railroad operated streamliners such as this between New York City and Chicago over the so-called water-level route. During the war years these same trains carried members of the armed forces under orders or on leave along with civilians, who were usually on the move for war-time business. It was the lucky GI who could get a seat on one of these streamliners, most of us usually got the mail train, which stopped at every station along the line. NYC RR

. . .

New England Commuter. Boston & Albany 4-6-6 tank engine, the steam version of the push-pull commute engine, is shown here taking a curve in the Boston area, date unknown. These specially built engines carried war workers to their important jobs in the Boston area during the hectic war years. RPS

U.S. Army Quartermasters Corps Plymouth construction type diesel pulling a large ATSF Automobile car down Private Right of Way next to Marina Blvd. heading toward the San Francisco Presidio Yards. This trackage was operated by the Army when this photo was taken in the late 1930s. It was an important link during the war years, allowing the Army to make up troop trains in the Presidio where they were handled by the California State Belt RR down the embarcadero, to the SP interchange. This rare photo was snapped by Warren Kendell Miller.

Steam, speed and smoke in New England. Boston & Albany #1441, a Berkshire type 2-8-4, clears a tunnel at high speed. Date of this photo is unknown. These heavy Berkshires (named for the Berkshire Mountains through which they ran) were a valuable asset to the war effort. RAIL PHOTO SERVICE OF MORAGA

· · ·

Erie #957. This 4-6-0 with a
commuter train at speed
somewhere in the wilds of
the Eastern seaboard. RPS

Erie Railroad #2915. Date
and location unknown. RPS

B&O #1—The Lord
Baltimore. This high-speed
4-4-4 pulled many a
passenger train over the
Baltimore & Ohio Railroad
during the war years. RPS

Central Railway of New Jersey commuter at speed across New Jersey. Camelback 680 roars down the right-of-way to her final destination. Note the baggage car on rear of train. RPS

Milwaukee Road's Polar Juice Jack #E-1. This excellent shot by W.C. Fancher shows this heavy electric in her heyday years. The Milwaukee Road climbed the Cascades of Washington with electric power rather than steam power. RPS

Service stop somewhere between St. Paul and Seattle. This is a typical troop train, note mixture of equipment used to make up this special troop train. No. 2587 gets serviced at this short stop. RNE

. . .

SP #2247. This old 4-6-0 hauled World War II freight trains over the light rail branch lines of the Southern Pacific. Note West Coast wartime visor over the headlight. The visor was used to keep the light limited to a small area. It was especially needed where the railroad ran along or near the coast, where the Japanese submarines were operating off the Pacific coast sinking ships within sight of land.

SP 1207. SP-designed yard goat at 3rd & Townsend passenger depot in San Francisco, Calif. These little pots did a herculean job when San Francisco and Oakland were the major Port of Embarkation for the Pacific war. WELCH PHOTO

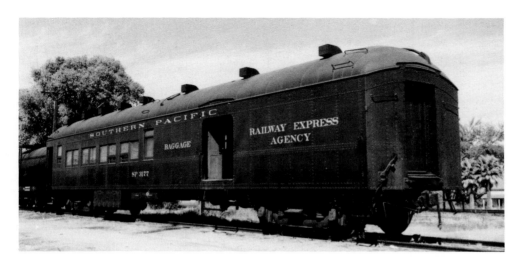

Heavy-weight combination passenger and express car. SP 3177 is a classic example of this little-known type of car used on the railroads throughout the country during the war years. Most of heavy steel construction, many were old-time wooden cars. This car was used on the Benson-Tombstone Branch Line in Arizona.

. . .

Tanks on the move. Highway traffic, along the Santa Fe Railway, halts at a safety guarded crossing while a long military train rushes to its destination. ATSF

SP 4147, as a helper-pusher, on a pre-war military train west of Truckee, Calif., in September 1941.
W.C. WHITAKER

SP 3701, 2-10-2, heavy drag hog that worked around the clock hauling war material to fill the holds of ships supplying the armed forces in the Pacific. The SP 3701 and her sister SP engines kept the supply lines open working day and night over the Sierras, across the high and low deserts through the valleys to their final destination—the ports of San Francisco, Oakland, San Pedro and Portland. RNE

SP 2461. Many years before the war, and the heavier engines used on the transcontinental route. This view shows Train #1 tooling across the Great Salt Lake. In later years this heavy 4-6-2 would be replaced by larger 4-8-2s and 4-8-4s. RNE

Passin' the Security Shack. Another great Warren K. Miller shot. Close at hand is the shack in which Private Miller and his buddies protected themselves from the harsh weather of the Sierras. In the background a SP-designed cab-in-front mallet pounds up the grade with a string of freight cars. During his duty at this lonely spot Private Miller only saw freights passing by; apparently most passenger trains hit this area during the night, thus he was unable to snap any troop trains. WARREN K. MILLER

SN #604-603 with #440 westbound downgrade through Pinehurst Canyon in the Oakland Hills. She has just come out of the tunnel from Redwood Canyon and is heading for the Oakland Army Base. Due to steep grades, freight trains through this area were quite small. This is rugged country within the Oakland City limits. September 1944. W.C. WHITAKER

Southern Railway four-car passenger train. Date unknown, but typical of heavyweight equipment used by the Southern Railway during the war years. ARR PHOTO BY C.W. WITBECK

Pounding down the main. War-time passenger train on the move. Pennsylvania Railroad #1361 on the head-end of a double-header, with a string of vintage day-coaches blasts her way up grade during those hectic days. RPS

Even the small trunk line railroad, such as the Western Pacific, had the big ones. No. 259, shown here, was used to pull the big drags up and down the Feather River Canyon in the Sierras. This excellent photo shows the 259 in all of her glory. RNE

And the Rocky Mountain connecting railroad needed the big ones. D&RGW 3706 picked up military material in Colorado and hauled it over the Rocky Mountains to Salt Lake City for its onward rush to the West Coast ports over the Western Pacific-Southern Pacific and Union Pacific. These giants indeed did their part in keeping the material moving. RNE

And they ran for the trains. Union Station, Omaha, Nebraska. Passengers checking in prior to boarding the "Shallenger" on its run out of Omaha in the early days of the war, before the big rush of troops and passengers that was to follow in the coming years. UPRR

Big switcher on the Pennsy. This 0-8-8-0 drag switcher was used throughout the war years by the Pennsylvania Railroad. RAIL PHOTO SOUVENIR OF MORAGA

GG-1 with passenger train at station. These top-line juice jacks keep the lines between New York City and the nation's capital open all through the war years. RPS

2
. . . .

The Fight for Freedom

"There is certainly no longer any doubt that we Americans are in for trouble. In whatever direction we look, trouble looms. It looms in Europe, where, nation by nation, Hitler is laying waste to the kind of life that we believe in. It looms on the Atlantic, where, whip by whip, the aid that we must send to Britain on the rim of freedom is being sunk. It looms in Asia, where, day by day, the threat of Japan comes closer. It looms at home where there are secret organizations—Communist, Fascist, Nazi—working behind the scenes. There is confusion in industry and transportation, inefficiency in Washington, doubt in the minds of the people, despair in the hearts of millions who are dedicated to liberation democracy. And out of it all, in the most desperate emergency that the democratic world has ever faced, come a trickle of airplanes, a trickle of ships, a trickle of munitions, and a trickle of hope. This is the state of the Union. We can understand what Hitler meant when he said that the U.S. would be the easiest country in the world to lick. If something is not done we shall lick ourselves."

EDITORS OF *Fortune Magazine*
July, 1941

While battles raged throughout Russia, the Baltic, Atlantic, and North Africa that summer of 1941, Americans for the most part were oblivious to the possibilities that they, too, might soon join in the fight for freedom. Armed with phrases like "mind your own business," most were concerned with the unusual heat that year, or who would make it to the World Series. Those with well-paying jobs were still trying to decide where to spend their two-week August vacations. The awful truth that they had to face, but which they were not facing, was that a world counterrevolution was in progress against the free way of life. Roosevelt knew that Hitler was not merely an ambitious dictator. He represented evil, a man determined to extinguish human liberty. The dilemma confronting Americans was that so long as liberty existed anywhere, Hitler must sooner or later attack it. That attack would at first be political and economic, but eventually it would be military. If his efforts failed and liberty continued to exist, Hitler would fail.

During that summer of 1941, lessons began pouring from the news media. They included:

1) So long as there was liberty in the United States, Hitler's ultimate objective must be the United States;

2) Americans must be willing to fight for freedom and the world must know that they were willing to fight, to the bitter end if necessary;

3) Only if there was a new world to create could Americans set forth fearlessly to give whatever that new world asked of them;

. . .
25

4) And, in the meantime, Americans had to prepare now for their possible participation in that fight.

But, said the editors of *Fortune Magazine*, "this nation of ours is still a democracy. And in a democracy leadership is competitive. Out of the issues with which we are faced today there will arise a new leadership, as gigantic as our land and as bold as our people. Let us hope that we may see these issues before, like China, we suffer defeat. Let us hope that we may see them before, like England, we are swept from the beaches of Dunkirk. But see them we must—and shall. The spirit of humanity still lives with us—the spirit of mankind struggling to be free."

ORGANIZATION FOR WAR

*I*n preparing for the possibility of war, the government figured that the railroads would be the most important segment of U.S. transportation, not only because they handled some 65 percent of the intercity freight traffic, but also because they were expected to have even more. If, for example, the Great Lakes steamers could not carry all the ore and coal through the locks in summer, railroads would have to haul some in winter. If America's trucks found themselves pressed to capacity, the rails would have to take over. When internal waterways became frozen, the burden would have to move overland. On top of this, the carriers were expected to share a tremendous amount of coastwise and intercoastal freight. Furthermore, they could even get some of the freight from the Orient that normally might go through the Panama Canal to the Atlantic Coast, but would be dumped in the Pacific Coast. All told, government statisticians figured the maximum possible diversion from ocean routes might conceivably amount to three million carloads annually. This by itself would not present the railroads with an impossible situation since the year before 36,400,000 carloads were hauled. However, added to an even greater increase in overland traffic, it would be reaching impossible levels.

As any railroader knows, three factors determine a railroad's capacity: (1) fixed plant, (2) rolling stock, and (3) motive power. America's fixed plants were certainly adequate. U.S. railroads had more main track than all continental Europe and Asia put together. Furthermore, railroad companies had enough motive power to handle all the cars they owned—at least for the coming year. The critical factor, according to

government officials, was the freight-car supply, which had to be excessive ten months of the year in order to make it through the months of September and October. The key question being asked in that summer of '41 was whether the railroads had enough cars to handle the fall peak without bringing about more than the routine, local shortages that generally take place even when there are plenty of cars. Budd commented, "If they have not, then priorities will have to be assigned to transportation. Non-defense producers will have to wait for their cars, and the fall peak will flatten out because there is nothing else for it to do. Can the railroads handle this fall's peak as it comes, without prolonging it, with the 1,850,000 usable cars in the lines? Everything depends on whether they can take on a million loaded cars a week for a few consecutive weeks. Although the A.A.R. early in the year (February 19, 1941) predicted total carloadings of some 41 million and a peak of 940,000 per week, present indications seem to justify the total of 44 million projected. By the end of the first six months the railroads had handled nearly 20 million; to handle 24 million in the last six months they will beyond all doubt have to take care of a million cars a week during the peak period. Outside observers who have analyzed the records doubted their ability to do so, while some car-service men, referring to the probability of using cars more intensively, are confident that they can."

And, of course, the car-service men were right. To be sure of their success, a series of steps was taken in the fall of that year.

The first was to buy all the cars that were being built. Budd estimated that private and contract car shops could produce a total of 175,000 new cars within the next twelve months since car builders now had A-3 priorities on steel. Furthermore, railroad companies could repair every old car not totally useless.

The second and third steps taken that fall of 1941 were to improve car utilization and cut out circuitous routing. The average car's capacity at that time was 49.7 tons, although it had been carrying only 27.6 tons, or 55 percent of capacity when loaded. During World War I, the average car was loaded to 68 percent of capacity. If the average car of 1941–42 were to be loaded in the same manner, it would carry 33.8 tons, and the usable car supply (1,600,000 railroad-owned and some 250,000 privately owned cars) would handle a weekly peak volume equal to more than 1,200,000 carloads. Not only this, but the average car moved only 2.5 hours a day—a relatively constant figure that had changed little in twenty years. According to an article entitled, "Transport: The Peak for Vic-

Busiest railroad terminal in the country during the war year—Pennsylvania Station, New York City. During the record year of 1945 more than 109,000,000 passengers passed through these hallowed walls. Pennsylvania Station was the starting point for long-distance travelers to Washington, D.C., and points to the south—Chicago, Indianapolis, St. Louis—and points as far west as San Francisco, Los Angeles, Portland and Seattle. It also served points north to Boston, and other New England cities, plus the local lines with its two Hudson River tubes to New Jersey and four tunnels under the East River to Long Island points as well as the Hells Gate Bridge up to Connecticut and Rhode Island. Eight hundred and fifty trains a day, including such famous name trains as the Broadway Limited-Trail Blazer to Chicago, the Spirit of St. Louis and Jefferson to St. Louis, the all-electric Congressional to Washington, D.C., just to name a few, passed through here. The station building, opened in 1910, occupies seven and a half acres of land on Manhattan Island, better known as downtown New York City. It has a main waiting room, 150 feet high by 110 feet wide and 300 feet long, whose design was inspired by the great buildings of ancient Rome. It was estimated that more than a half million persons, either as train passengers or visitors, passed through this station each day of the week during those confused war years. All trains operated underground on different levels, no train appeared on the surface at the Pennsylvania Station. PRR

. . .

The juice jacks that moved war material on the East Coast. Here is a line of Pennsylvania Railroad's famous GG-1s ready to be dispatched for whatever assignment given them, be it military cargo, troop trains or regular civilian train service. These electric engines operated between New York City, Philadelphia, Washington, D.C., and Harrisburg. The engines were 79 feet, six inches long, weighed 477,000 pounds and had a 4-6-6-4 wheel arrangement. They operated on electric power received via pantographs from 11,000 volt catenary wire system overhead, they are at 4,620 continuous hp. and for short periods, when hauling heavy loads on a grade, can develop as much as 8,000 hp. The engines can pull a passenger train of 14 cars at 100 mph and freight at 50 mph. PRR

M-3 tanks being unloaded
for the 3rd Army Maneuvers
at Boyce, La., in August
1942. It was hot and heavy
work for both trainmen and
GIs to get these monsters on
and off the flat cars. Due to
extensive trackage of the
railroads from 1941-45, they
were used extensively to
move heavy equipment.
USASC

Somewhere along the Santa
Fe Railway's track these
scout tanks, part of a heavily
laden military train, pause
briefly in their swift race to a
port of embarkation. This
scene shows the changing of
the guard at one of the trains
rest stops. ATSF

Vehicles such as tanks and
guns are moved on flat cars.
This shot, taken somewhere
in Southern California,
shows the method of moving
military trucks long
distances. SPRR

tory," that appeared in *Fortune Magazine* during August of 1941, the carriers had been obtaining more miles per car per day by running trains faster and not by cutting down standing time of cars. But such statistics were deceptive. Cars were loaded to 68 percent of capacity of 1917 and 1918 primarily because they carried heavy wartime freight. Cars averaged only 2.5 hours a day in motion because they had to spend a great deal of their off-season time waiting around in yards for demand. At that time, shippers or consignees were getting two free days in which to load or unload. After that, they were penalized only $2.20 a day for four days and after that $5.50 a day.

In the late 1930s, the shipper was allowed to select his own routes, regardless of how circuitous they might be. This was by law. If he chose, he could dispatch freight from Boston to Chicago by direct routes (some 900 miles), or indirectly via Savannah (2,000 miles). If a shipper wanted to save on storage charges, he would obviously choose the longest possible route between any two points. Not only this, but a railroad company that had no specific orders from the shipper could go in for some circuitous routing of its own. Actually, it was under little compulsion to short-haul itself. For example, it could have freight originating on its line so as to produce maximum revenue—even if it turned the goods over to a connecting line at a point farther from the destination than the loading point.

There were other steps to be taken by America's railroads for the possibility of war besides buying all the cars that could be built, improving car utilizing, and cutting our circuitous routing. These included flattening out the fall peak, ordering more locomotives, improving fixed plants, pooling facilities, getting more labor, pooling passenger runs, and coordinating transportation with trucks.

The most pressing of these steps were the order of

more locomotives and improving fixed plants. In the fall of 1941, 36,000 of the 41,000 locomotives in America were in a good state of repair even though most dated before World War I. Government statisticians figured that since one modern locomotive could do as much as three or four ancient teakettles, a proportionately greater number would not be needed to increase loadings to 49 or 53 million. But it was hard for Budd to see how the nation's railroads could get along on less than 1,200 new engines in both 1942 and 1943. Actually, he hoped for 1,400 new locomotives a year. By June 1, 1941, America's railroads received 218 since the beginning of the year and had another 517 on order. Everyone agreed that the nation had enough locomotive-building capacity, although it needed priorities on steel castings and forgings. The Lima Company's output of 500-plus duplicate-design engines was not affected by rearmament. And, while Baldwin and American gave up most of their facilities for building locomotives, each company was still producing over 300 a year, while General Motor's Electro-Motive Corporation built some 350 diesels a year.

Budd said at the time these steps were being taken, "There is perhaps no more intricate job, and some calling for abundant and objective judgment, than the hitherto completely neglected task of delimiting the proper field of each branch of American transportation. Today it must be done. Otherwise the nation will not get the most in transportation for the smallest possible application of time and manpower, the two elements of which there never will be enough."

Of course, Budd's dreams of emergency transportation reforms could not be easily accomplished under a competitive peacetime setup. Nor could they take hold overnight. But Budd was certain that railroad and government leaders endowed with the power to enforce decisions would be up to the job ahead of them.

Here two heavy steam engines on the waiting track are ready to make their runs. No. 4306, left, is a heavy freight drag engine, while the 3672 is a high-stepping passenger train engine. PRR

Troops hanging out the windows of an old coach. Army band playing for them as train departs from staging area en route to Boston Port of Embarkation. USASC

Unloading a brand-new White Motor Coach in 1945 at the Key System Yards, Oakland, Calif. RNE

Nite sleeper. This Pullman Company streamlined sleeper car (#106), delivered to the Southern Pacific Railroad in February 1941, was the counterpart of the daylight cars. This two-tone gray car was built specially for the "Lark," which ran the same line as the Daylight but at night. She was well broken-in for wartime service. SPRR

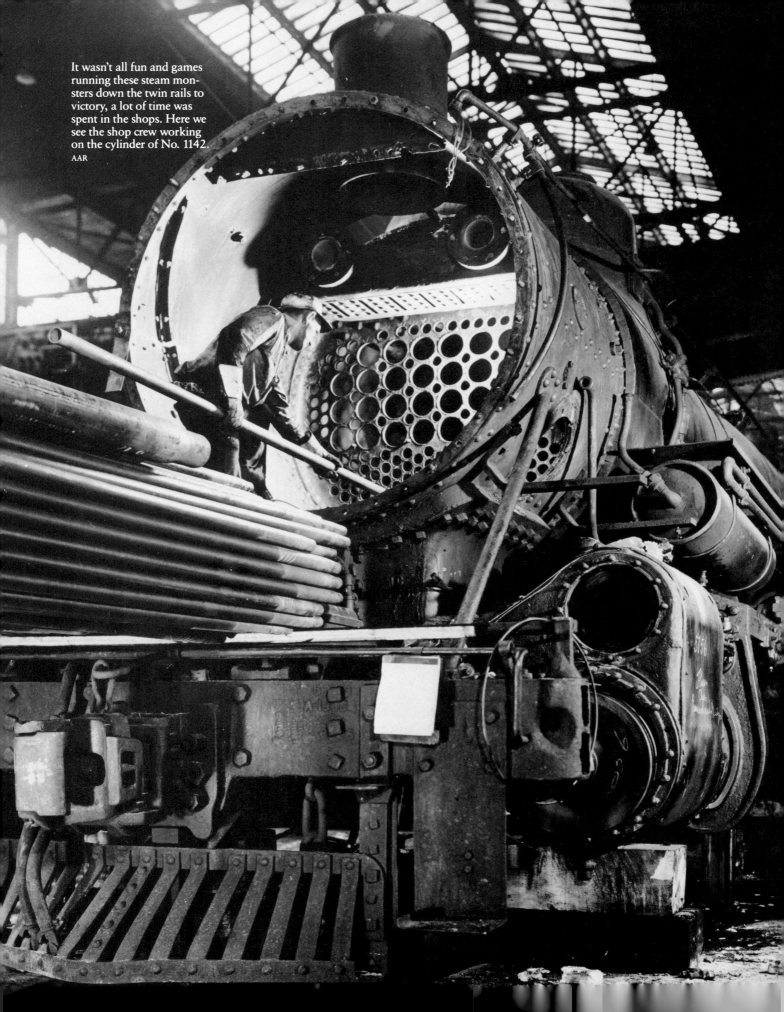

It wasn't all fun and games running these steam monsters down the twin rails to victory, a lot of time was spent in the shops. Here we see the shop crew working on the cylinder of No. 1142. AAR

Erection shop at Sacramento is the locomotive hospital. sp

This view at the Roanoke Shops of the N&W gives you an idea of the size of these heavy-duty loco-motives. N&W

*D*uring 1941–42 America had to deal with the most vital problem of transportation that ever confronted a nation—the problem of railways providing enough service to enable that nation and her allies to win a victory in the first "all-out" worldwide war. That year witnessed the greatest voluntary cooperative effort ever put forth by private industry in any country. As mentioned, it was an effort of railroad management and shippers to make available adequate equipment for all the military and civilian demands to the railway plant, which had just suffered from a decade of depression. In magazines and journals such as *Railway Engineering and Maintenance, Railway Age, Railway Mechanical Engineer, Railway Signalling,* and *Railway Electrical Engineer* that appeared in 1941–42 the story of making railway service adequate is told in feature stories, editorials, and advertising pages. The records of railway performances are shown below:

Selected Operating Statistics

First 10 Months of 1942-1941

	1942	1941	Inc. or Dec.	% Change
Locomotive klms. (total)	32,627,238	31,198,127	+1,429,111	4.6
Freight train klms.	13,717,028	13,016,815	+700,213	5.4
Passenger train klms....	8,828,323	8,917,810	−89,487	1.0
Mixed & Specl. klms.....	3,103,711	3,051,897	+51,814	1.7
Non-revenue klms.	107,907	62,801	+45,106	71.8
Total train klms.	25,756,969	25,049,323	+707,646	2.8
Passenger car klms.	69,225,261	67,804,618	+1,420,643	2.1
Freight loaded klms.	208,788,725	190,073,319	+18,073,406	9.5
Freight empty klms.	93,317,760	92,128,606	+1,189,154	1.3
Freight total klms.	302,106,485	282,843,925	+19,262,560	6.8
Net-ton klms. (1,000s) ..	5,678,253	5,007,532	+670,721	13.4
Gross ton klms.	12,857,994	11,740,080	+1,117,914	9.5
Total No. cars loaded...	417,980	397,438	+20,542	5.2
Averages				
Net tons per train klms..	394	366	+28	7.7
Gross tons per train klms.	852	818	+34	4.2
Speed per hr. (klms.) frt.	21.6	23.3	−1.7	7.3
Gross ton klms. per train hour	18,382	19,046	−664	3.5
Utilization of tractive power	76.5%	74.2%	+2.2%	3.0
Frt. Loco. klms. (daily).	185	185	....	..
Liters oil per 1,000 G. T. K. (frt.)	41.9	42.6	−0.7	1.6
Per cent loaded car klms. to total	69.1	67.4	+1.7	2.5
Car klms. per car (daily)	57.1	62.0	+4.9	7.9
Net tons per car........	27.2	26.1	+1.1	4.2
Cars on line daily	17,389	15,018	+2,371	15.8
Klms. line operated	11,765	11,639	+126	1.1

—Freight Locomotive Utilization for Twelve-Month Period

	Total freight locos. 1	Un-service-able 2	Stored service-able 3	Active 4	Active locos., per cent total locos. 5	Aggregate tractive force (000) 6	Loco. miles (000) 7	G.t.m. (excl. loco. and tender) (000,000) 8	Freight-train miles (000) 9	Loco. miles per active loco. 10	Loco. miles per total locos. 11	Loco. miles per freight train mile 12	G.t.m. per 1,000 lb. trac-tive force (000) 13	G.t.m. per train mile 14
1941														
November	21,774	4,350	1,049	16,375	75.2	1,500,393	56,893	106,241	49,924	3,474	2,613	1.14	70.8	2,151
December	21,776	3,406	1,071	17,299	79.8	1,501,223	57,323	102,957	50,231	3,256	2,632	1.14	68.6	2,073
1942														
January	21,888	3,253	926	17,709	81.0	1,503,056	59,461	106,532	51,930	3,358	2,717	1.15	70.8	2,075
February	21,841	3,238	916	16,687	81.0	1,503,449	55,030	100,489	38,031	3,111	2,520	1.15	66.8	2,115
March	21,920	3,141	740	18,039	82.3	1,505,308	62,087	117,851	53,124	3,442	2,832	1.15	78.2	2,200
April	21,915	3,119	688	18,108	82.6	1,506,402	62,128	120,725	53,921	3,431	2,835	1.15	80.2	2,264
May	21,963	2,995	612	18,356	83.6	1,507,934	65,385	130,070	56,558	3,562	2,977	1.16	86.2	2,325
June	21,927	2,888	549	18,490	84.3	1,513,015	63,292	125,959	54,711	3,423	2,887	1.16	83.3	2,328
July	21,923	2,744	527	18,652	85.7	1,513,670	66,197	132,089	57,193	3,548	3,020	1.16	87.1	2,336
August	22,028	2,844	475	18,709	85.0	1,515,741	67,389	135,972	58,136	3,602	3,059	1.16	89.8	2,366
September	22,075	2,705	367	19,003	86.1	1,518,757	66,716	134,166	57,625	3,511	3,022	1.16	88.3	2,356
October	22,027	2,344	340	19,343	87.8	1,532,031	70,461	141,880	60,717	3,642	3,198	1.16	92.6	2,365

Statistical data from same source as that in Table I.

—Freight Locomotive Utilization During October Traffic Peaks

	Total freight locos. 1	Un-service-able 2	Stored service-able 3	Active 4	Active locos., per cent total locos. 5	Aggregate tractive force (000) 6	Loco. miles (000) 7	G.t.m. (excl. loco. and tender) (000,000) 8	Freight-train miles (000) 9	Loco. miles per active loco. 10	Loco. miles per total loco. 11	Loco. miles per freight train mile 12	G.t.m. per 1,000 lb. trac-tive force (000) 13	G.t.m. per train mile 14
1923	33,203	5,947	1,865	25,391	76.5	1,793,785	65,973	92,640	58,492	2,600	1,990	1.13	51.6	1,584
1924	33,359	6,079	3,219	24,061	72.5	1,832,216	62,910	94,730	55,952	2,610	1,880	1.12	51.6	1,693
1925	32,390	5,423	3,055	23,812	73.5	1,827,207	65,568	100,026	58,512	2,760	2.020	1.12	54.7	1,709
1926	31,543	4,782	2,699	24,062	76.5	1,842,369	66,031	107,238	58,798	2,740	2,100	1.12	58.3	1,824
1927	30,960	4,626	3,418	22,916	74.0	1,815,903	64,231	105,797	56,582	2,800	2,070	1.13	58.5	1,870
1928	30,062	4,764	2,971	22,327	74.2	1,796,379	65,165	110,276	57,211	2,920	2,160	1.14	61.2	1,928
1929	28,912	4,477	2,680	21,755	75.5	1,768,968	64,756	110,444	56,748	2,970	2,240	1.14	62.2	1,946
1930	28,738	5,123	4,940	18,675	65.3	1,775,435	54,665	94,931	46,313	2,920	1,910	1.18	53.3	1,965
1931	28,667	6,071	6,225	16,371	57.3	1,755,779	44,903	75,403	40,250	2,740	1,560	1.11	42.8	1,873
1932	27,310	7,891	5,801	13,618	50.0	1,719,166	40,372	66,143	36,344	2,970	1,480	1.11	38.4	1,820
1933	26,925	8,985	3,787	14;153	52.8	1,672,763	40,589	65,812	36,476	2,860	1,510	1.11	39.4	1,804
1934	25,964	8,707	3,402	13,855	53.7	1,597,000	41,205	66,311	37,159	2,960	1,585	1.11	41.3	1,785
1935	25,144	8,414	2,213	14,517	57.9	1,572,950	45,151	75,671	36,858	3,120	1.800	1.22	48.2	1,895
1936	24,498	6,813	1,642	16,043	62.9	1,571,487	50,742	86,987	44,333	3,170	2,070	.114	55.3	1,948
1937*	23,889	5,914	1,673	16,302	68.4	1,558,838	50,117	88,245	44,572	3,070	2,100	1.12	56.5	1,998
1938*	23,729	7,300	1,785	14,665	61.9	1,566,246	44,622	79,951	39,615	3,040	1,880	1.13	60.0	2,036
1939*	22,909	6,425	832	15,652	68.4	1,550,988	49,945	93,209	44,034	3,190	2,180	1.12	61.4	2,120
1940*	22,186	5,253	1,352	15,581	70.4	1,517,597	49,983	92,946	44,272	3,200	2,249	1.12	61.2	2,183
1941*	21,830	3,528	841	17,461	79.5	1,499,817	61,501	116,340	53,866	3,522	2,812	1.14	77.6	2,183
1942*	22,027	2,344	340	19,343	87.8	1,532,031	70,461	141,880	60,717	3,642	3,198	1.16	92.6	2,365

* Data from I. C. C. Bureau of Statistics, Freight Service Operating Statistics of Class I Steam Railways in the United States (Statement No. M-210, to and including 1935); Freight Train Performance of Class I Steam Railways in the United States (Statement No. M-211 OS-A, 1936 to date); and Motive Power and Car Equipment of Class I Steam Railways in the United States (Statement No. M-240 OS-F). Aggregate tractive force based on A. A. R. Car Service Division Form CS-56A-1.

Expenditures for Maintenance of Way and Structures, Class I Railways

(Thousands)

	Average 1925-1929 (Inclusive)	1932	1933	1934	1935	1936	1937	1938	1939	1940	1941
Superintendence	$57,262	$36,552	$31,921	$33,347	$35,605	$37,357	$39,801	$38,935	$39,072	$40,231	$43,407
Roadway Maintenance	83,698	32,042	30,026	30,714	35,809	38,289	42,017	37,219	36,112	38,372	47,923
Tunnels	2,608	1,466	933	1,051	1,453	1,326	1,709	1,256	1,210	1,374	1,780
Bridges, culverts, etc.	43,471	19,434	17,627	20,139	22,646	24,032	26,268	24,200	24,782	26,514	31,754
Ties	114,859	50,294	43,543	50,748	51,936	56,315	59,799	53,762	59,910	58,353	64,928
Rails	47,402	13,762	14,324	15,418	16,302	21,192	20,412	17,406	22,065	22,736	24,684
Other Track Materials	48,354	15,726	15,362	18,694	20,959	26,732	30,228	22,817	29,670	33,428	38,711
Ballast	19,379	4,969	5,814	7,538	8,357	11,992	12,362	7,744	10,343	11,592	15,093
Track Laying and Surfacing	211,067	83,407	77,025	85,641	94,033	106,072	121,113	103,420	114,932	117,839	156,142
Fences and Snow Sheds	5,831	2,135	2,047	2,412	2,260	†3,397	†3,689	†2,939	†3,235	3,408	3,930
Crossings and Signs	13,115	6,468	5,969	7,293	7,186	*	*	*	*	*	*
Buildings	79,000	24,924	24,576	31,448	33,047	41,252	47,757	34,315	41,018	46,852	60,412
Water Supply	10,444	3,952	3,749	4,441	4,497	5,860	6,182	4,672	5,207	6,020	6,736
Tools and Equipment	18,230	7,917	8,051	10,666	11,044	13,452	15,408	11,456	13,720	15,434	18,971
Injuries	5,907	2,811	2,417	2,810	2,727	3,118	3,303	2,806	2,929	3,220	3,547
Removing Snow, Ice and Sand	9,947	4,699	4,188	5,630	7,001	13,365	6,655	5,239	6,110	9,030	5,995
Miscellaneous	78,449	40,621	34,714	37,310	39,105	51,059	58,891	51,961	56,516	29,202	79,076
	$849,021	$351,179	$322,286	$365,300	$393,967	$454,810	$495,594	$420,147	$466,831	$497,031	$603,088

Note; Miscellaneous includes signals and interlocking, all charges for depreciation and unclassified items.
* Not shown separately since 1935.   † Includes signs, as well as fences and snow sheds.

The Pattern of Freight-Car Demand—1941-1942

(Carloadings, in thousands, by Commodity Groups in Quarters)

Commodity group	First Quarter			Second Quarter			Third Quarter			Fourth Quarter			Annual Totals		
	1941	1942	Inc. or dec. (−)	1941	1942	Inc. or dec. (−)	1941	1942	Inc. or dec. (−)	1941	1942*	Inc. or dec. (−)*	1941	1942*	Inc. or dec. (−)*
Grain and grain products	411	512	101	493	468	−25	621	609	−12	498	575	77	2,022	2,164	142
Live stock	139	149	10	142	157	15	152	179	27	217	256	39	650	742	92
Coal	2,000	2,036	36	1,481	2,136	655	2,071	2,091	20	2,038	2,094	56	7,590	8,356	766
Coke	180	184	4	155	183	28	171	180	9	172	186	14	678	732	54
Forest products	496	577	81	539	645	106	600	672	72	549	549	..	2,185	2,443	258
Ore	170	190	20	902	1,014	112	985	1,139	154	626	686	60	2,682	3,029	347
Miscellaneous	4,027	4,613	586	4,671	4,909	238	4,811	5,165	354	4,926	5,042	116	18,436	19,730	1,294
Total car loads	7,423	8,261	838	8,383	9,512	1,129	9,411	10,035	624	9,026	9,388	362	34,243	37,196	2,953
Merchandise l.c.l.	1,964	1,892	−72	2,081	1,395	−685	2,006	1,142	−864	1,991	1,168	−823	8,041	5,597	−2,444

* Last two weeks of 1942 estimated.

Miles of New Lines Completed in the United States Since 1830

Year	Miles	Year	Miles	Year	Miles	Year	Miles
1830	40	1886	8,400	1863	574	1919	686
1831	99	1887	13,081	1864	947	1920	314
1832	191	1888	7,066	1865	819	1921	475
1833	116	1889	5,707	1866	1,404	1922	324
1834	214	1890	5,739	1867	2,541	1923	427
1835	138	1891	4,620	1868	2,468	1924	579
1836	280	1892	4,648	1869	4,103	1925	644
1837	348	1893	3,024	1870	5,658	1926	1,005
1838	453	1894	1,760	1871	6,660	1927	779
1839	386	1895	1,420	1872	7,439	1928	1,025
1840	491	1896	1,692	1873	5,217	1929	666
1841	606	1897	2,109	1874	2,584	1930	513
1842	505	1898	3,265	1875	1,606	1931	748
1843	288	1899	4,569	1876	2,575	1932	163
1844	180	1900	4,894	1877	2,280	1933	24
1845	277	1901	5,368	1878	2,428	1934	76
1846	333	1902	6,026	1879	5,006	1935	45
1847	263	1903	5,652	1880	6,876	1936	93
1848	1,056	1904	3,832	1881	9,789	1937	148
1849	1,048	1905	4,388	1882	11,599	1938	38
1850	1,261	1906	5,623	1883	6,819	1939	58
1851	1,274	1907	5,212	1884	3,974	1940	26
1852	2,288	1908	3,214	1885	3,131	1941	54
1853	2,170	1909	3,748			1942	74
1854	3,442	1910	4,122				
1855	2,453	1911	3,066				
1856	1,471	1912	2,997				
1857	2,077	1913	3,071				
1858	1,966	1914	1,532				
1859	1,707	1915	933				
1860	1,500	1916	1,098				
1861	1,016	1917	979				
1862	720	1918	721				

The Railroads Prove Their Economic Virility

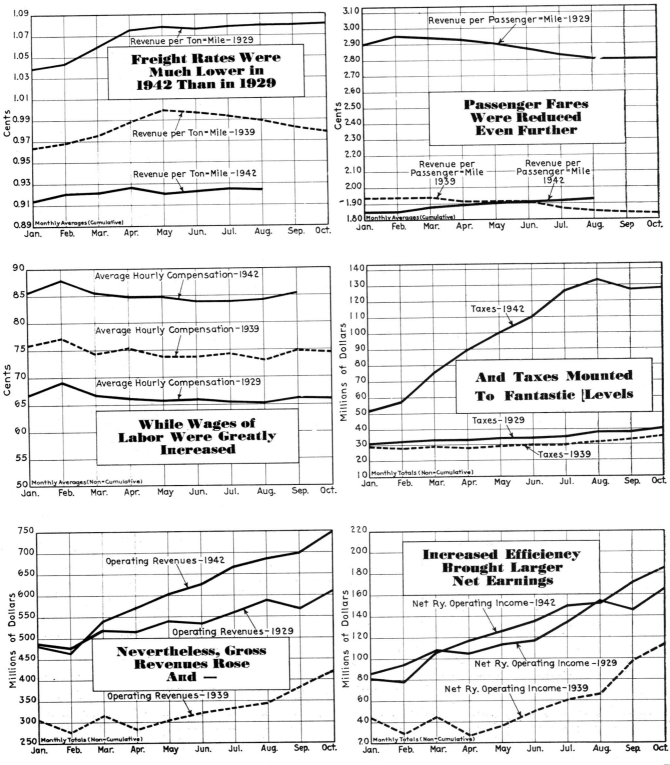

. . .

36

Earnings of "Large Steam Railways", Ten Months, 1942, 1939 and 1929

Name of Railroad	OPERATING REVENUES					NET FROM RAILWAY OPERATIONS					NET RAILWAY OPERATING INCOME				
	10 Months 1942	% 1942 of 1939	10 Months 1939	% 1942 of 1929	10 Months 1929	10 Months 1942	% 1942 of 1939	10 Months 1939	% 1942 of 1929	10 Months 1929	10 Months 1942	% 1942 of 1939	10 Months 1939	% 1942 of 1929	10 Months 1929
Alton	25,323,765	185	13,723,013	104	24,440,232	9,124,205	275	3,321,957	154	5,922,760	3,869,828	634	610,062	128	3,028,425
Atchison, Topeka & Santa Fe	291,408,561	219	132,837,663	156	187,316,840	129,142,274	450	28,688,337	193	66,826,856	64,522,435	416	15,495,344	128	50,564,603
Atlantic Coast Line	90,567,757	232	39,016,907	147	61,470,417	39,013,269	444	8,785,318	235	16,632,830	17,015,217	566	3,003,673	149	11,414,490
Baltimore & Ohio	251,481,658	193	130,116,497	120	208,988,441	83,307,273	249	33,501,285	146	57,110,542	48,834,937	237	20,626,698	112	43,514,963
Boston & Maine	64,341,833	168	38,245,901	97	66,100,250	23,375,405	215	10,871,431	138	16,917,001	11,823,018	214	5,537,605	105	11,312,177
Central of Georgia	23,554,837	184	12,812,702	111	21,194,133	8,006,482	477	1,677,710	159	5,048,852	5,923,425	1199	494,194	156	3,797,105
Central of New Jersey	47,707,864	173	27,512,110	98	48,845,992	15,252,786	205	7,453,734	113	13,529,291	7,479,458	499	1,497,417	95	7,903,032
Chesapeake & Ohio	150,553,937	155	96,978,245	139	108,521,975	71,577,174	177	40,392,460	194	36,862,219	30,388,688	105	28,972,622	96	31,753,845
Chicago & Eastern Illinois	19,367,301	153	12,625,585	90	21,504,399	6,292,262	227	2,777,137	127	4,937,761	2,954,554	425	695,988	144	2,057,791
Chicago & North Western	113,828,627	157	72,725,178	86	132,416,763	35,707,062	291	12,262,137	99	36,104,993	20,740,086	470	4,410,742	82	25,220,388
Chicago, Burlington & Quincy	132,541,814	167	79,366,486	97	137,340,527	52,450,128	264	19,867,719	117	44,864,733	28,424,261	318	8,944,883	92	31,010,846
Chicago Great Western	20,894,948	139	15,043,115	96	21,699,570	7,399,721	178	4,163,190	151	4,900,197	2,618,438	208	1,260,681	112	2,336,749
Chicago, Mil., St. P. & Pac.	146,589,748	166	88,565,051	100.2	146,232,065	50,414,122	305	16,520,797	136	37,108,559	27,385,497	519	5,279,839	119	23,104,477
Chicago, Rock Island & Pac.	110,180,964	168	65,744,688	89	124,362,010	41,790,776	324	12,890,182	125	33,399,540	29,952,853	697	4,298,018	142	21,150,752
Chicago, St. Paul, Minneap. & Omaha	19,306,093	131	14,686,523	84	22,925,843	4,763,618	218	2,180,268	96	4,939,194	2,615,828	...	−62,552	85	3,087,196
Delaware & Hudson	38,134,788	181	21,037,847	109	34,692,507	13,494,750	204	6,609,079	172	7,841,075	7,789,333	170	4,573,964	112	6,937,867
Delaware, Lackawanna & West'n	60,170,503	145	41,572,633	88	68,677,667	19,900,412	205	9,700,908	98	20,291,993	9,382,111	196	4,777,556	64	14,590,234
Denver & Rio Grande Western	43,137,889	210	20,515,545	149	28,906,893	17,813,241	500	3,560,844	209	8,516,419	14,340,565	158	912,597	199	7,214,422
Duluth, Missabe & Iron Range	39,370,602	241	16,351,408	149	26,506,750	26,353,656	287	9,185,289	164	16,028,529	7,024,211	99	7,047,289	52	13,623,318
Elgin, Joliet & Eastern	28,162,177	202	13,966,337	124	22,725,865	10,867,982	268	4,058,801	125	8,699,344	2,744,020	125	2,192,967	51	5,343,121
Erie	110,906,130	166	66,706,045	115	96,636,135	40,455,241	226	17,928,843	185	21,848,408	20,379,351	214	9,510,219	121	16,838,708
Grand Trunk Western	25,226,000	144	17,526,921	131	19,237,428	6,861,828	246	2,791,560	135	5,090,730	4,522,678	592	763,694	148	3,055,879
Great Northern	135,473,817	174	77,812,867	125	108,459,226	58,424,946	219	26,679,048	161	36,320,158	31,829,813	193	16,481,492	115	27,564,789
Gulf, Mobile & Ohio	26,999,719	174	15,493,722	126	21,381,576	10,291,279	262	3,928,835	178	5,794,840	4,447,372	257	1,730,985	123	3,612,453
Illinois Central System	173,963,450	190	91,515,621	114	152,577,703	63,257,602	266	23,772,139	119	35,333,577	31,823,535	228	13,954,590	136	23,395,911
Lehigh Valley	63,659,486	170	37,403,124	105	60,902,083	22,459,643	221	10,155,613	140	16,099,732	10,070,245	178	5,669,969	88	11,453,539
Louisville & Nashville	136,892,998	189	72,241,062	122	112,246,823	55,472,276	291	19,072,479	241	22,997,047	19,629,229	154	12,767,450	114	17,251,536
Minneapolis, St. P. & S. Ste. M.	35,648,571	151	23,660,294	86	41,609,946	10,488,086	192	5,454,164	89	11,724,200	6,588,444	263	2,509,155	85	7,723,235
Missouri-Kansas-Texas Lines	45,303,904	191	23,669,442	96	47,199,742	13,853,563	277	5,000,413	92	15,120,511	7,634,615	657	1,161,321	76	9,997,758
Missouri Pacific	143,799,935	210	68,536,290	122	118,335,835	61,638,819	434	14,192,413	193	31,908,249	41,298,902	767	5,383,471	195	21,173,815
New York Central	486,556,328	175	278,363,006	145	335,472,661	156,183,327	226	69,011,812	187	83,480,571	70,531,750	248	28,418,491	123	57,442,306
Pittsburgh & Lake Erie	28,430,525	189	15,019,849	97	29,237,347	8,711,996	405	2,151,311	166	5,263,485	5,427,179	214	2,538,117	78	6,981,639
New York, Chicago & St. Louis	72,617,115	207	35,122,521	150	48,320,461	34,228,525	295	11,616,222	232	14,727,457	11,769,428	179	6,583,987	123	9,601,860
New York, New Haven & Hartford	127,908,081	186	68,663,202	108	118,103,310	51,471,288	296	17,383,936	130	39,621,239	24,444,705	400	6,108,805	89	27,390,967
Norfolk & Western	115,366,165	153	75,320,244	118	97,974,149	51,830,617	157	32,974,731	121	42,726,174	18,958,568	77	24,517,200	52	36,492,357
Northern Pacific	95,650,986	179	53,300,916	117	81,918,915	32,595,807	300	10,881,359	147	22,221,430	21,917,621	290	7,569,613	120	18,333,374
Pennsylvania	691,505,861	199	347,951,655	117	579,372,182	235,763,900	238	99,090,619	140	168,630,145	115,570,557	198	58,374,098	97	118,760,552
Long Island	29,082,150	133	21,837,963	83	35,131,457	8,000,052	140	5,718,282	65	12,268,686	1,988,200	499	398,360	25	7,918,561
Pere Marquette	35,927,151	147	24,444,010	86	41,754,328	9,458,074	183	5,174,594	70	13,497,006	5,023,527	211	2,377,381	54	9,359,168
Reading	84,734,211	184	46,145,495	104	81,110,480	31,757,695	231	13,756,998	178	17,830,736	17,478,186	193	9,579,793	123	14,236,416
St. Louis-San Francisco	68,673,145	181	37,869,994	96	71,867,708	23,995,843	406	5,906,146	109	21,975,476	19,867,537	70	2,825,483	110	18,004,741
St. Louis, San Francisco & Tex.	2,740,836	207	1,322,397	168	1,631,717	1,303,034	519	250,988	348	374,462	913,183	....	−88,281	1239	73,712
St. Louis Southwestern Lines	38,850,091	242	16,077,892	176	22,050,510	19,641,935	619	3,171,416	380	5,170,711	7,590,262	1026	739,709	240	3,156,957
Sea.oard Air Line	87,857,870	244	35,987,329	180	48,930,636	35,361,258	598	5,910,876	271	13,035,578	24,360,868	1111	2,193,040	268	9,101,069
Southern	165,590,286	204	81,368,761	137	120,847,693	71,533,014	285	25,093,983	205	34,972,807	32,814,375	203	16,187,495	126	26,003,566
Southern Pacific	296,064,001	214	138,253,377	154	192,111,347	117,223,511	305	38,388,169	184	63,559,046	59,580,350	317	18,816,182	139	42,863,939
Texas & New Orleans	80,640,119	225	35,799,350	129	62,693,221	38,144,626	419	9,101,250	227	16,779,663	18,699,134	400	3,895,230	184	10,142,596
Texas & Pacific	40,693,804	187	21,733,253	106	38,541,924	16,838,905	273	6,168,707	141	11,936,776	9,341,750	240	3,533,703	123	7,580,773
Union Pacific System	276,434,724	203	136,261,385	148	187,379,396	100,165,691	279	35,867,289	165	60,675,589	42,046,081	294	14,291,276	107	39,207,256
Wabash	64,098,273	176	36,473,384	98	65,691,005	25,313,015	310	8,152,472	141	17,903,834	7,389,625	317	2,327,869	63	11,819,153

Nearly eight months after Pearl Harbor, the U.S. Army had yet to deliver an offensive land attack on an enemy anywhere. It had, by the fall of 1942, more than 3,500,000 men in uniform organized into nearly 80 divisions. The Air Force was ready with 225 battle squadrons. Actually, the U.S. Army Air Force was girdling the globe. The army thus far had carried the offensive to the enemy only by air. It was doing so from bases in the Middle East, India, New Guinea, Australia, China, the Aleutians, Hawaii, and, since July 4, the British Isles. This simultaneous operation on all fronts everywhere was a novel form of warfare, never practiced by the Germans or Russians. The defensive bases already set up by the United States along both coasts of the Western Hemisphere, across Africa and in the North Atlantic, ran into staggering numbers. Perhaps these new methods of dispersed air attack would work.

However, on the ground, the men and officers of the huge U.S. Army were rarin' to go. Many were already stationed in Northern Ireland, England, Iceland, Greenland, Egypt, India, Australia, New Guinea, New Caledonia, the Aleutians, Bermuda, and Trinidad. Except for the airmen and a few soldiers who escaped from the Philippines, they had never seen the enemy. Meanwhile, the greatest battles of history were being fought between the axis and the Soviets on the blood-drenched fields of southern Russia.

Meanwhile, the Allies were massing troops and materials. The commander of all U.S. forces in Europe, Lt. Gen. Dwight D. ("Ike") Eisenhower, was preparing the first major American assault. Ike knew that his Americans were not yet prepared to smash the German army and could well lose the first battle. He was determined to hit the Germans where, when, and how it would hurt them the most. Asked for a July 4 message in 1942, he said, "No time for messages until we can say them with bombs and shells."

If there was to be a second front in late 1942 or early 1943, everything hinged upon getting the supplies and troops to the forward staging areas. And, that, or course, meant the railroads must do their jobs.

By the end of 1942, no U.S. industry astonished its partisans and critics, as well as itself, more than the railroad industry. A year after the outbreak of war across two oceans, the nation's railroads had met every demand asked of them. Also, they had met a great many demands that no one thought they would have to meet. For example, they, and not the U.S. Navy, prevented the Nazi submarine program from cashing in on the terrible success that it was. Laughed at for suggesting they could probably haul 200,000 barrels of oil and gas a day from the Southwest to the East, the carriers were hauling nearly 900,000 barrels, some two-thirds of the normal demand, by December 1942. As a result of performances like this, the railroad companies afforded the government neither a reason nor an excuse to take them over as a war measure.

The carriers had achieved this by utilizing plant and equipment to an incredibly high degree. As the statistics above suggest, in the first seven months of 1942, ton-miles were about 33 percent above those of 1929, the previous high. Yet, the means for handling this remained considerably under former peaks. For example, the number of employees was 20 percent below that of 1929; the number of freight cars (and aggregate capacity) was about 20 percent below that of 1929; aggregate locomotive tractive force (pulling power) was 19 percent below that of 1920. The carriers were now compelled to improve this record in order to keep it clean. Some railroad experts anticipated a 20 percent to 25 percent increase in 1943's freight and passenger volume. But, being realistic, the most they could hope for in new equipment was a five percent addition to the 1,981,000 freight cars in line; only two percent to the 41,500 locomotives, and nothing to the 28,000 passenger cars. In 1929, the carriers consumed over eight million tons of finished steel as equipment, rails, and supplies. In 1942, they received less than two-thirds of that amount, and no one dared guess how little the railroads would receive in 1943. However, everyone expected more intensive fusion, coordination, and utilization of the carriers during the coming year.

In November of 1942, *Fortune Magazine* carried an article entitled, "How the Railroads Did It," describing in detail how "They've been squeezing a lot more out of everything they own than they ever have before, and they'll have to squeeze even harder." According to that article, the critical transportation problem two years before was the impending shortage of railroad freight cars. It was then possible to make out a "watertight" case for the proposition that the carriers could not haul what they were indeed hauling by the fall of 1942 without owning 500,000 more cars. Actually by Sept. 30, 1942, the railroads owned less than 100,000, more than they had twenty months before. The story of how they got along without the other 400,000 is amazing.

That article in *Fortune* pointed out that transportation is a three-dimensional operation, involving time as well as weight and distance. That was why the small cargo plane, which carried only a few tons, could produce a large number of ton-miles per hour. And, that was why a railroad could do wonders in utilizing boxcars simply by moving them faster. In 1920, except for a few passenger runs, speed was not known on the railroads. A few felt it was uneconomic. As the years passed, and as the trains ran heavier and heavier, they were run faster and with fewer delays. In 1920, the average freight train produced 7,303 net ton-miles per hour (or hauled 730 pay tons at ten miles an hour, or 365 tons at twenty miles an hour). By 1939, with faster and heavier trains, the figure was 13,450. By late 1942, it was over 15,000. Thus, because of the recent transcontinental movements of military and other heavy material, hauls were longer. And, because of the delay often inherent in loading and unloading, a car whose time was devoted to long hauls could produce more ton-miles than one whose time was devoted to short hauls. There was no question that old railroad habits were being changed, and especially by the government, which had considerable control over them. In 1940, for example, the various railroad companies and the Association of American Railroads working alongside of thirteen regional Shippers' Advisory Boards (which had been established primarily to estimate carloadings) tried to encourage shippers to load cars closer to capacity. Later, this partnership created Vigilance or Car Efficiency Committees to oversee carloading practices, as well as to suggest improvements. Virtually all the shippers responded. One steel company, for example, found that it could load its coal cars heavier by attaching vibrators to the cars and shaking down the load. And some carriers showed gratifying increases in the underloaded less than carload (l.c.l.) category.

Around this time, the Office of Defense Transportation issued Order No. 1. Joe Eastman's office forced railroads to load l.c.l. freight cars to at least six tons (the figure eventually was raised to ten tons) and was without a doubt a much-needed step in car utilization. Generally, l.c.l. traffic accounted for less than two percent of all ton-miles, but used 14 percent of boxcar capacity (in terms of boxcar-days). In 1939, it averaged less than five net tons per car, against an average of 26.5 tons for all boxcars. In the week ending Sept. 12, 1941, it required 159,000 cars. But in the week of Sept. 12, 1942, it took less than 80,000 cars for about the same tonnage. In short, the order increased the total available boxcar supply some ten percent.

Virtually all railroad men were happy with Joe Eastman and his extremely competent Office of Defense Transportation. Endowed with enough power to rule a small country, Joe was nonetheless discreet and low-keyed. Yet, he was not a shrinking violet. Railroaders respected these qualities. For instance, ODT Order No. 18, primarily designed to save motive power, required all cars (other than l.c.l.) to be loaded to visible capacity if freight was light, or to load limit if freight was heavy. If a shipper loaded, say, forty tons instead of twenty tons into a car weighing twenty tons, the total drag on the engine was sixty tons, against eighty tons if the load was carried in two cars. At first, shippers were angry with Order No. 18. How on earth were they to weigh a car if there were no scales within twenty or thirty miles? But ODT persisted in its requirement, thereby helping the motive power situation when a while later it became acute.

Two views of troops standing in night formation before loading onto the Union Pacific Railroad cars in this September 1944 shot. UPRR

. . .

NORTH PLATTE CANTEEN

North Platte, Neb. The rush is on. The train has just
stopped and the GIs knowingly run to the canteen
entrance in the railroad station. UPRR

Facing page bottom: The girls get into the act. Union
Station, Omaha, Neb., canteen. Here service people, both
men and women, relax while waiting for their train. UPRR

This train did not stop long in North Platte, Neb., just enough time to be serviced by the Union Pacific Railroad's service gang, so you had to move fast (run was the word) to the canteen, grab a fast bite and get back aboard the train or get left behind. UPRR

Union Station, Omaha, Neb., canteen reading room for the GIs. UPRR

A tribute to the ladies of all those railside canteens. Here the volunteer ladies of North Platte, Neb., waiting for the next train with its cargo of GIs. These ladies, who met every train that passed through their city, were always ready with hot coffee, cold drinks, doughnuts, homemade cookies and sandwiches for the tired serviceman. UPRR

Bringing goodies out to the GIs who couldn't get off the train. The ladies of North Platte, Neb., certainly did their part in making the transcontinental trip as pleasant as they could. UPRR

THE ROLE OF THE SOUTHERN PACIFIC IN 1942

*D*uring the early months of World War II, everyone agreed that the most crucial sector of the home transportation front was the Southern Pacific Company. Because the railroad was the strategic segment of the transcontinental supply line, the operations of U.S. railroads as a whole were also the operations of Southern Pacific, some 15,600 miles of track sprawled across most of western America. A two-billion dollar corporation employing 86,000 people, Southern Pacific in mid-1942 was already doing 136 percent more business than in 1939. More than 86 percent of Southern Pacific was single track running across the prairies, through the deserts, and over mountains, a geography that represented some of the greatest operating difficulties in the nation. Those within government circles felt that whether the government would take over America's transportation system during the first six months of World War II would depend on how well Southern Pacific handled the record flow of traffic on its rails.

Like most of our American railroads, Southern Pacific was producing more ton-miles in the fall of 1940 than it was in the corresponding period of 1929. During the next year, it was producing more than half again as much freight transportation as in the fall of 1929, with less motive power and fewer cars. Since Pearl Harbor, it had moved tremendous amounts of military equipment in extra and regular freight trains, and hundreds of thousands of soldiers in more than a thousand special trains. By the end of March 1942, when the average U.S. railroad was amazed to find traffic at about the 1929 level, the Southern Pacific had produced 88 percent more ton-miles and 54 percent more passenger-miles than it had produced in the first quarter of that great 1929 year.

"All this the S.P. has done," said *Fortune Magazine* in a 1942 article entitled, "They're Crowding the Rails," "if not with timetable dispatch, then with a new alacrity and even exultation. 'So this is the business they said was dying!' is the motto that might be tacked in every executive den, yard office, and roundhouse. The whole organization of 75,000 is on its toes, delighted and amazed by the realization of its capacity. The minor operating officials, a breed of men who just naturally live and dream railroading, are luxuriating in a continuous round of duty. Traffic men, bursting with bitter pride, never tire of pointing out that the S.P. is taking everything handed it, often by ship-

pers who previously disdained to ship by rail, without imposing priorities and without benefit of Defense Plant Corporation."

There was little question that the Southern Pacific was rolling again. In the early months of World War II, the company had to borrow or lease twenty-four engines from other railroads and to reconcile shippers and passengers to long delays. For example, in February 1942, 50 percent of the regular through-

Pre-war troop movement from California to Fort Lewis, Wash. They brought their own entertainment. A pause on the long train ride shows the troops at a rest stop somewhere on the Southern Pacific Railroad. SPRR

Another view of the troops having their mess at their Pullman seats. Note that they kept their gear with them on the train. SPRR

Observation car of the Daylight. Delivered in December 1939 this observation car carried many a serviceman during the days of World War II between San Francisco and Los Angeles.
SPRR

Daylight Limited Day Coach, built in 1939. Coaches of this design along with the combination car— the diner—the lounge/observation car that made up this greatest of all daytime streamliners did their job well during the war years running up and down the Pacific Coast between Los Angeles and San Francisco.
SPRR

For the lucky ones who were able to secure a seat on the Daylight Limited between San Francisco and Los Angeles, it was a pleasure trip, especially during the war years. Here we have combination car 3303 delivered to the Southern Pacific in December 1939.
SPRR

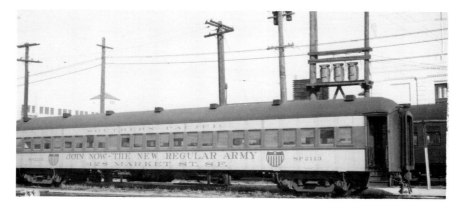

SP Coach 2113 was used to advertise the U.S. Army. Many railroad cars such as this were used to advertise the military services throughout the country.

. . .

S.P. 1806, another small branch line engine. These light 2-6-0s certainly did their share of moving the freight in the hectic days of World War II. RNE

SP 5039, 4-10-2, pulling out of a Southern California freight yard with a full consist of freight cars. This is a heavy drag engine used in the deserts of Southern California and Arizona. RNE

passenger trains had been late at their destinations, while only a fraction of the freight trains had made running time.

The company's responsibility was made more difficult by a variety of factors. The most important, of course, was the mushrooming industrial development at Los Angeles, San Diego, Portland and the SF-Oakland Bay area. This consisted primarily of aircraft factories, aluminum and magnesium plants, steel mills, shipyards, and new mining operations. Just two years before, none of these had been in existence. A second major hurdle for Southern Pacific to overcome was the increase in traffic resulting from a shortage of ships. Generally, the railroad faced heavy water competition from both the Pacific Coastwise and Panama Canal shipping. By 1942, virtually all coastwise commercial shipping had disappeared, allowing the Southern Pacific to pick up and carry the oil, gasoline, and pulp. Millions upon millions of tons of intercoastal commercial freight no longer passed through the Panama Canal. From the west coast, lumber, paper, and canned goods moved east over the transcontinental rail. However, the critical question that no one wanted to discuss dealt with what would happen if the canal was bombed and the Southern Pacific and other carriers had to handle all the military traffic.

Yet another factor making the company's responsibility more intensified during 1942 was the huge military and naval program developing all along the west and gulf coasts. That program consisted of camps, airfields, forts, cantonments, arsenals, embarkation ports, and supply-line bases—all of which the Southern Pacific served more than any other railroad. Added to this program was the incredible movement of arms and military supplies made in the Atlantic states.

Today, upon reflection of the role played by America's railroads during World War II, most carriers would agree that the burden fell more noticeably on Southern Pacific in 1942 than upon any other railroad company. Well developed and superbly managed during the early years of its history, the Southern Pacific was able to function beautifully when the chips were down. For example, $150 million was plowed back into its property between 1929 and 1940. Furthermore, the company's founders believed in Jim Hill's precept to refrain from double-tracking to any extent and build alternate main lines into new territory. Southern Pacific never went in for excess capacity and therefore was able to fend off receivership.

But, the company's lines were located in some of America's most rugged terrain and during that critical 1942 year, many wondered if the railroad would do

SP's greatest passenger train—the Daylight Limited. In the eyes of many, the most beautiful passenger train in the country. This excellent view taken along the Pacific Ocean above Santa Barbara, shows the northbound train headed for San Francisco. The Daylight ran in two sections, the regular Daylight left in the morning, while the noon Daylight left Los Angeles and San Francisco at noon. This view shows the engine in its two-tone orange Red & Black boiler. Engines used on the Daylights were 4-8-4s in the 4410-series. RNE

the job in a territory studded with natural barriers.

In its brilliant analysis of the Southern Pacific in 1942, *Fortune Magazine* described how mountain track, besides being more costly to build and operate, had a fraction of the capacity of level track—a major point when troops and war materials were being rushed over it. *Fortune* pointed out that curves were often so sharp that a locomotive could not run fast uphill even if the load allowed. The Southern Pacific grades were so steep that locomotives could not maintain a high average without an uneconomical use of motive power. As a rule in the early 1940s, a locomotive needed four times the motive power to haul a train up a one percent grade (one foot rise in a hundred) as on absolutely level track, and eight or nine times as much up a two percent grade. Southern Pacific's largest cab-in-front articulated locomotives could roll as high as 6,000 tons at 50 miles an hour over a fairly level division. But three were pressed into service to wrestle 4,350 tons at 16 miles per hour up the two-and-a-half-percent grade through Emigrant Gap. And, when one adds seven mainline summits involving grades of more than two percent, the concern of railroad and government officials is apparent. On top of this, such curves and summits meant a demand for more power, the wearing down of wheel flanges and rails, increased possibilities for derailment, and heavy weather conditions.

The prime objective of wartime transportation in 1942 was to get maximum tonnage over the line with a minimum of time, men, and motive power. Southern Pacific, like all the other railroad companies of America, approached that task with confidence. The biggest hour in its history, Southern Pacific was convinced that it could handle anything the government wanted. Not only was the company going all out for victory in this total war, but was also going to demonstrate that the government need not bother with controls. Certainly, everyone agreed, Washington, D.C., wasn't interested in operating Southern Pacific, or the other carriers. The only possible advantage in government control was that it would equalize traffic and equipment more drastically than the carriers were likely to. However, Southern Pacific and the other companies were determined to obtain unheard-of production from their plants. Perhaps the best example of that attitude was a choice made by Northern Pacific in April of 1942. Although hard-up for motive power itself, the company sent Southern Pacific five large locomotives direct from the Baldwin Works because Southern Pacific needed them most.

Indeed, if there was a pressing need at Southern Pacific, it was for locomotives. When war broke out, the company had to immediately rent seventeen engines from the various carriers at the price of one mill per pound of tractive force per day. Returning five of them in March 1942, the company rented another 12. By late that year, Southern Pacific was squeezing as high as 20,000 miles a month out of each engine, an average of nearly 700 miles a day for passenger locomotives and 6,000 miles a month out of freight locomotives. In April less than five percent of the roster (an all-time low) were laid up for repairs. "The company's motive-power department had rehabilitated everything that looked and acted like a locomotive including teapots more than fifty years old," commented *Fortune*.

Of course, like those of other railroad companies, roundhouses throughout the system were on a full three-shift basis for repairs, and the shop force, swollen by 43 percent, was on a 48-hour week. As the shops received more and more mechanics, there was talk of going on a three-shift basis, as well as possibly going over into the munitions work. Meanwhile, the company was persuading the A.F. of L. to shelve the agreements on promotion of apprentices and helpers to mechanics, thus providing 20 percent more mechanics. On top of all this, Southern Pacific was adopting various work shortcuts, such as "turning" locomotive tires without mounting them on lathes. With this type of technique, cutting tools were substituted for the brakeheads and the engine was pulled slowly up and down the tracks. The tools chiselled away and restored the contours of the wheel tires. Such a job took only a day or two compared to a week to drop the wheels and mount the tires on lathes. Hundreds of locomotive-hours a year were saved.

"Despite all this," commented an official, "the S.P.'s record depends on what it can expect in new locomotives. It can congratulate itself on what it already has. Its expenditures for equipment and improvements during the lean years have been notably generous. Since Aug. 1, 1939, the S.P. has ordered locomotives and cars worth $82 million, roughly equal to its total net income from 1930 to 1941. Included in this figure are 252 locomotives worth nearly $40 million, of which all save seventy should be delivered by this summer of 1942 with forty promised beginning in the early Fall. Not counting the forty, the S.P. lines will have about 9% more tractive force on hand this Fall than last Fall. If the forty come through in time for the Fall peak, the total increment will be 14%. But the freight traffic will probably be at least 20% above the 1941 level in the Fall. Can the S.P. handle 20% more traffic with at best 14% additional power? Everyone of our personnel says yes."

And, of course, history demonstrates how accurate that response was. This happened because of a number of reasons. One of the most important was that each new locomotive could more than displace its equivalent tractive force in old engines. This was obvious. Because it developed more horsepower per pound of tractive force, because it ran farther without refueling, a new passenger engine exerting 75,000 pounds of tractive force would accomplish twice and three times the work of an older engine with only a rating of 37,000 pounds.

SP 4313, a beautiful 4-8-2 before they spoiled her looks with a shroud on top of the boiler, coming in on Train #9, the Fast Mail, at the Oakland Mole. Note that the train is made up of Mail & Express cars with a few passenger cars on the rear end. This was the "slow" train that carried the bulk of the mail in the pre-airline days. RNE

Southern Pacific 4-10-2 No. 5000, the largest non-articulated series on the SP, is met by officials and workers upon its arrival at the Sacramento Shops prior to the war. RNE

. . .

Arrival of SP's #5004 — another 4-10-2 — at Sacramento, Calif., before World War II. These mammoths of the iron pulled more than their weight in tonnage across the deserts of California and Arizona in those hectic World War II days. RNE

Lots of action at the Southern Pacific Railroad yards, Indio, Calif., on a cool day shortly after Pearl Harbor. This scene, taken on December 16 less than two weeks after the war had started, shows the importance of the railroad in moving this much-needed equipment on the West Coast. USA 161ST SIGNAL PHOTOGRAPHIC CO.

1942: The Year All Railroad Records Were Broken

*T*he railroads-in-war news in January 1943 announced that traffic in 1942 was the heaviest that any form of transport ever moved. Dr. Julius H. Parmelee, Director, Bureau of Railroad Economics of the Association of American Railroads, wrote, "During this first complete year of direct participation by the United States in the present world conflict, many outstanding developments affected the railways, their traffic, their plant, and their personnel. Although many powerful things occurred, none was more important than the unprecedented volume transported without congestion."

And, of course, he was right. As mentioned before, the total volume handled by the carriers was 630,000,000 ton-miles. This was 155,000,000,000 ton-miles (nearly 33 percent greater than that handled in 1941) more than the previous record year. Freight loadings approximated 42,800,000 cars, an increase of 510,000 cars above 1941. At the same time, railroads established a new high record in volume of passenger traffic in 1942. Passenger-miles (the number of passengers multiplied by the distance carried) totaled 53,000,000,000. This exceeded by more than 6,000,000,000 passenger-miles, or 13 percent, the previous record established in 1920. It also exceeded 1941 by more than 23,000,000,000 passenger-miles, or 80 percent. Naturally, part of this heavy passenger traffic in 1942 was attributed to troop movements, over 2,000,000 transported monthly in organized movements.

J. J. Pelley, President of the Association of American Railroads, commented, "There were other outstanding efficiency records established by the railroads in 1942. Among the most noteworthy were:

1) Average load of freight per train was 1,030 tons, the highest on record. In 1941, it was 915 tons.

2) Performance per freight train more than doubled, gross ton-miles per freight train hour having increased from 16,555 in 1921 to 35,874 in 1942, while net ton-miles per freight train hour increased from 7,506 in 1921 to 16,216 in 1942.

3) For each pound of fuel in freight service in 1942, railroads handled 9.2 tons of freight and equipment per mile compared with 6.2 tons in 1921.

4) The average load per freight car was 31½ tons in 1942, the highest on record.

5) The average haul of freight shipments in 1942 broke all records, increasing by some fifty miles compared with 1941.

6) Average daily movement of freight cars was 49 miles in 1942, a new high record, and an increase of 90% compared with 1921.

7) Average passengers per car and per train broke all previous records by a wide margin, the load per car being more than 40% and the load per train being more than 60% greater than in 1941.

8) Average capacity of freight cars were 50½ tons in 1942, the highest on record.

9) Average daily movement of freight locomotives in 1942 was 122.5 miles, or an increase of 57% compared with 1921.

10) Tractive power of locomotives averaged 52,000 pounds, an increase of 40% compared with 1921."

Indeed, such statistics were astonishing, even to railroaders. There is little question that the carriers did an excellent war job in 1942. That story consisted primarily of accomplishment and preparation: accomplishment in moving the greatest volume of freight and passenger traffic in world history without serious shortage or congestion; and, preparation for the still-greater volume of traffic demand in 1943. The questions on everyone's mind were how much greater would that 1943 demand be, and would the railways be able to supply it satisfactorily? Railroads in the first eleven months of 1942 installed in service 60,789 new freight cars and 668 new locomotives. For 1943, the War Production Board promised 20,000 new freight cars and 386 new locomotives, including both steam and diesels. Would these be enough? Certainly for the coming year's fighting the rail carriers would again have to exercise the greatest efficiency. However, it seemed reasonable to conclude that on the basis of the 1942 performance the job would again get done. Pelley commented, "This will be true not only in 1943 as it was in 1942, but will run also throughout as many more and later years as the present conflict may continue."

3

The Military Railway Service

Any book dealing with America's railroads and their role in World War II must include a chapter dealing with soldier-railroaders. It is a little-known story, long forgotten by now, and rarely described, although 43,500 troops (out of 16,535,000) were assigned to the various units of the Military Railway Service. Providing superb technical service, these men from all sections of the Operating Departments of the railroads, were organized into units corresponding to the divisional organization of a railroad. They operated the railroads in the war zone, and, as nearly as could be done, railroaded in the American tradition.

Before beginning this brief segment, it is interesting to note that by the end of 1953, 30,910,000 Americans had participated in the nine major wars, which the United States had fought between 1775 and 1954. Of course, there were no troop trains in the Revolutionary War, War of 1812, and the Mexican War (although there were some rail movements in this war). During the Civil War, some 2,192,000 fought for the North and the Military Railway Service forces numbered 24,964. In World War I, 4,744,000 Americans participated, with over 83,000 men organized into 51 M.R.S. units in France. The Allied Armies of World War II needed much more logistical support per man than all the other armies in American history. Most of the 43,500 railroad men utilized in World War II were experienced railroaders who had been employed by the carriers. Because of their experience, they were able to maneuver through incredibly complex freight handling problems.

On Dec. 7, 1941, the Military Railway Service was well organized on an inactive duty basis, with the majority of officers for each unit selected, commissioned, and assigned. On the roster were ten Railway Grand Divisions, fifty Railway Operating Battalions, and ten Railway Shop Battalions. Key non-commissioned personnel were already enlisted in the Organized Reserves. At that time, War Department policies provided for age-in-grade for officers. For original appointment, officers were to be between the age of 21 and 60, except that lieutenants and captains were not to be over 45, majors and lieutenant colonels 55, and colonels 60. Before all of the units were organized, a modification of the age-in-grade was made because in most instances competent experienced Trainmasters, Roadmasters, Road Foremen of Engines, and Round House Foremen, although physically fit, were in excess of the minimum age for the grade by regulations.

Railway Grand Divisions, consisting of a Railway Grand Division Headquarters, two or more Operating Battalions, and a Railway Shop Battalion, were organized primarily on a geographical basis. As these divisions were called into active service and began their training period, they were an integral part of the basic M.R.S. organization and functioned accordingly.

On March 15, 1942, the 727 R.O.B. (Southern Railway Company) was called into active duty, the first units to be called after the declaration of war. The next activated were the 713 R.O.B. (Sante Fe) and the 753 R.S.B. (Cleveland, Cincinnati, Chicago, and St. Louis Railway); then Headquarters, M.R.S., and the 730 R.O.B. (Pennsylvania Railroad), on May 15. It was decided that the Headquarters of the M.R.S. would be at Fort Snelling, Minn.

In general, sponsoring railroads provided technical training for their own units. For example, the Southern Railroad sponsored the 727 R.O.B. for training on the line of its railroad between Meridian, Miss., and New Orleans, La. The unit was camped at Camp Shelby, Hattiesburg, Miss. Often, such battalions as the 727 connected their encampments together and used the constructions as training. Lines would be surveyed, grades and curvatures considered, track laid, bridges built, and locomotives provided.

During August of 1942, America's Military Railway Service received its first overseas assignment: to unravel the transportation and construction problems in Alaska. From higher authority, General B.B. Somerwell, Commanding Army Service Forces, received the order, "Proceed by first Air Priority to White Horse, Yukon Territory, and after consultation with General Hoge take over by lease the White Pass and Yukon Route, retaining it as a Class 1 carrier and retaining the civilian personnel augmenting with military material, equipment, and personnel sufficient to handle the military traffic."

Within the coming months and the next few years, other such orders would be commonplace. The Military Railway Service would be called upon to handle rail operations in North Africa, between 1943–1944; Iran, 1942–1945; India, 1943–1945; the Philippines, New Caledonia, Australia, and Japan, 1942–1945; Sicily and France, 1943–1945; Northern and Southern France and Belgium, 1944–1945; and Germany, 1944–1946. The accounts of railroading operations in these countries would fill another volume. However, the few photographs shown here testify to the Service's remarkable achievements. One example was the Allied invasion of Sicily in 1943. In this instance, a fast build-up of rail capacity was absolutely essential. Troops landed in Sicily on the morning of July 10, while an advance party of railroaders landed two days later. General George S. Patton said, "Within 24 hours after landing, supplies were being moved by rail to the Third Division." At Salerno, near Naples, with the Germans only thirteen miles away, railroad operations began. After the enemy was driven back to Caserta, the M.R.S. began transporting 4,700 tons per day. Within a week of Operation Overlord, D-Day, on June 6, 1944, cars and locomotives brought from England were at work carrying munitions as far as Carentan, over 30 miles away.

By August 7, M.R.S. was able to achieve an astonishing rail capacity of 3,000 tons daily. Rapid expansion then was the rule. Daily average rail movement increased to 5,000 tons between August 27 and September 30, and then to 7,000 tons through November of 1944. Steadily increasing as the armies advanced was the length of haul from the ports. By the end of November, some 15,000 tons of freight daily were being delivered by rail east of Paris. This was only 120 days after the St. Lo break-through. When one considers how the rails had been badly damaged by Allied bombings and German demolitions, one can't help but be amazed at the accomplishment. Further-

more, many of those rails were still under attack. By Christmas, the figure reached 23,000 tons daily.

There is no greater example of how indispensable the M.R.S. was in World War II than in how it supplied General Patton. Most readers remember the famed Red Ball Express, that brilliantly organized and operated truck transport system which handled 7,000 tons daily. With Patton pursuing retreating German armies, Red Ball had to follow, often handling operational gear on roads stretching 400 miles and more. But the mileage turnaround from Cherbourg to Liege was 1,044. The need for railroads was apparent. General Somerwell, commander of the Army Service Forces, said, "The trucks, of course, required a tremendous amount of gasoline. Their payload over such a long distance was relatively small. We always felt that if the effort up there was to be of any size, it would have to be supplied by railroad."

The Allied Armies were winning the war and it was partly due to the fact that America had the finest railroaders in the world supplying the needs of those armies. The brilliance of the railroaders, both in terms of officers and engineers, was unequalled in know-how and competence. Carl R. Gray Jr., the Director-General of the Military Railway Service from 1942 through 1945, summed it up best when he said, "Our railroaders in the M.R.S. are patriotic true Americans and may be counted upon to respond to a call to duty in any further difficulties that require their service. There is no surer way to succeed than to get a man who knows how to do a job, give him the responsibility and authority, and then support him. This was the secret of success of the M.R.S. in World War II."

Firing up an Army steam locomotive. Army personnel ran the railroads on military bases. USA

Steam locomotive #6994 was built by Lima Locomotive Works for the U.S. Army in March 1942. This view was taken at the Lima Works at Lima, Ohio, when the locomotive was turned over to the Army. USA

"General Pershing" USA #8341. Last of the World War vintage steam engines in March 1942. This engine served in both wars with a good record. USA

U.S. Army Quartermaster Corps #7532 75-ton Army steam locomotive, after being repaired at the Holabird Quartermaster Depot in Baltimore, Md., in April 1937, saw duty in many World War II operations. USASC

The Navy operated all types of rail equipment. Here we have a small center cab diesel, built by Porter, working tank cars of oil that were being interchanged to the Naval Operating Base from the Virginian Railway at Sewalls Point, Va. USN

US Army switcher 7450. This type engine was used on various military bases, and after the war sold to both common carrier and private railroads. USA

THE ALASKA RAILROAD DURING WORLD WAR II

Reprinted from RAILS ACROSS THE TUNDRA *by Stan Cohen*

*E*ven before the attack on Pearl Harbor, the Alaska Railroad was intimately involved in building Alaska's defenses. With the establishment of military bases in Anchorage and Fairbanks in 1940 and 1941, the railroad experienced a dramatic increase in its haulage. At the same time, the railroad found it increasingly difficult to obtain labor due to increased military activity in Alaska and the Lower 48.

The increase in traffic and the inconvenience of shuffling staff members from the terminal site to the federal building prompted the railroad to begin construction of a three-story depot and general office building in Anchorage. It was completed in 1942 and is still in use today. To alleviate a bottleneck in traffic on the Kenai Peninsula, the railroad in 1941 also began construction, at a cost of $5.3 million, of that spur to the Passage Canal known as the Whittier Cutoff.

When the United States entered the war, the railroad became even more closely involved with Alaska's defense. Alaska was put under control of the Army, while the railroad was watched by civilian guards placed at strategic points along its route. A bypass was built around the famous "loop" to speed the flow of goods and as a precaution against enemy air attacks. A blackout rule, put in force throughout the state, made wintertime train operations hazardous.

The war also caused the railroad to undergo a labor shortage as many of its employees joined the military or left for higher-paying jobs. This problem was compounded by a critical shortage of locomotives and freight and passenger cars. Finally, the Alaska Defense Command loaned some soldiers to keep the trains operating and additional rolling stock was brought in, some of it from the defunct Copper River and Northwestern Railroad.

But these measures were not enough. By early spring 1943, it was obvious that something had to be done to keep the railroad operating in a safe and efficient manner. Help was on its way in the form of the 714th Railway Operating Battalion, a part of the U.S. Army Transportation Corps.

Activated at Camp Claiborne, La., in March 1942, the battalion was made up for the most part of experienced railroad men from the Chicago, St. Paul, Minneapolis and Omaha Railroad. It was ordered to travel to Ft. Lewis, Wash., to pick up additional track-maintenance personnel, and it headed for Alaska with a total of 23 commissioned officers, two warrant officers, and 1,092 enlisted men.

The battalion landed at Seward on April 3, 1943, and immediately went to work to augment the railroad's slim civilian workforce. Maintenance was at a low ebb, and, due to the manpower shorage, there was a tremendous backlog of material piled up at Seward.

The opening of the port of Whittier later in 1943 alleviated some of this backlog and another aid came in 1943 with the arrival of six new locomotives, built by Baldwin for use overseas and numbered 551 to 556, similar to the 500-class locomotives already in service on the Alaska Railroad. Still, the men of the 714th had all they could contend with trying to run the railroad in tough winter conditions with barely enough personnel to do the job.

The Army also supplied soldiers for another vital railroad activity. A coal shortage developed in Alaska during the war due to the military's demands for fuel and the lack of miners to supply it. Thus the Army sent soldiers to keep the railroad's Eska coal mine open between 1942 and 1945.

During the war, Army personnel in Alaska sometimes stayed at the McKinley Pass Hotel, which had been taken over by the Army as a recreation camp. The railroad operated a Brill car and trailer to the hotel from Anchorage, making a round trip each week.

In the aftermath of the expulsion of the Japanese from Alaska in 1943, the military relaxed a little, and its presence began to diminish in the territory. The War Manpower Commission recruited more civilian workers for the railroad in early 1945, and the 714th was released in May of that year.

With the end of the war, the railroad returned to its prewar schedule. The war had been an exhausting trial for the railroad, and considerable capital was needed to bring it back to safe operating conditions. But, with its return to a civilian role, the railroad knew it had contributed in its own way to the war effort.

Soldiers operating the Alaska Railroad had a unique PX (post exchange). Most PXs were in a fixed location but this wasn't practical for soldiers of the railroad unit, assigned to duty along the 500 miles of track in the Alaska Railroad. The PX sold personal necessities and minor luxuries such as toilet articles, cigarettes, candy and magazines.
USA SC337850 & SC176686

An Army MT boat, one of the shallow draft tugs used in rafting operations on the Tanana River, just brought in on a flat car of the Alaska Railroad, sits on a siding at Tanana, Alaska. USA SC207110

General view of the Whittier area on June 7, 1943. A train is hauling MT boats and fuel trucks. AMHA

A winter scene of the Whittier area showing the dock, fuel tanks and buildings. Whittier is in a heavy snow belt of Alaska. AMHA

Maj. Gen Simon Buckner and party at the tunnel entrance preparatory to setting off the blast that would open the Alaska Railroad's cut-off tunnel to Whittier. AMHA

An Army inspection party including Maj. Gen. Simon B. Buckner (second from right on the right row) in his private railroad coach on the way to Whittier. USA SC396826

View of the upper end of the
Whittier townsite. AMHA

The Whittier railroad
station, May 1944.
USA SC571430

Steam locomotive unloading
at the Whittier dock, 1942.
AMHA, ALASKA RAILROAD
COLLECTION

THE ALASKAN WHITE PASS
AND YUKON ROUTE

The United States' entry into World War II and the decision to build the Alaska (Alcan) Highway had a profound effect on the White Pass Route. The highway was to be built from Dawson Creek, British Columbia, to Fairbanks, Alaska, through the Northern part of British Columbia, the Southern Yukon and the interior of Alaska.

It was to be a rush project designed to meet a real threat to Alaska by Japanese forces in the early days of the war. The inland route was selected because it was out of range of Japanese air and naval forces and crossed less-rugged mountains than those of the coast. This route also would connect a string of air bases stretching from Edmondton, Alberta, to Fairbanks, Alaska.

The road was to be built by American troops with American money through mostly Canadian territory in order to permit overland shipment of war material to Alaska and Northern Canada.

The 1,500-mile route provided only three main access points for the thousands of men and tons of material building up in the South.

One was Dawson Creek, British Columbia, at the southern terminus of the road. Dawson Creek was the end of the Northern Alberta Railroad and was connected by road to Edmonton, Alberta, and points south. The second was Fairbanks, the northern terminus of the highway. Fairbanks was connected to Anchorage and the sea by the Alaska Railroad and the Richardson Highway.

The third was Whitehorse, the terminus of the most important link to the interior of the Yukon: the White Pass Route from Skagway. Men and materials could be shipped up the inside passage to Skagway, hauled on the railroad to Whitehorse, and then sent north and south along the highway.

In addition to supplying the Alaska Highway project in 1942–43, the railroad carried material for the CANOL construction project, a road and pipeline built by the U.S. Army from Norman Wells, Northwest Territories, to pipe oil to a Whitehorse refinery used by the military.

Construction of the highway began in March 1942, and it was determined at once that help was needed to keep the trains running.

Although the railroad could handle peacetime demand, it was overwhelmed by the quantity of material needed for the two construction projects. The docks at Skagway and the railroad's equipment were both inadequate. Most of the equipment, left over from the Gold Rush days, was practically worn out. Fewer than a dozen engines were in working order, and the roadbed was desperately in need of repair.

So the railroad was leased to the U.S. government for the duration of the war, and the U.S. Army took over its operation, retaining the civilian employees. The 770th Railway Operating Battalion of the Military Railway Service officially assumed control on Oct. 1, 1942, and operated the White Pass Route until the war was over. Most of the men in the battalion were from Southern states, and on their official introduction to the North country they encountered one of the worst winters in its history. Construction was started on many buildings and shops in Skagway and Whitehorse to accommodate the troops and material being assembled for construction of the road.

Rolling stock was built at the repair yards in Skagway, and even one of the old locomotives that had run to the Klondike gold fields was pressed into service.

Engines Nos. 10 and 14 were shipped north in 1942 by the Army. They had been built originally for the East Tennessee and Western North Carolina Railroad. Engines Nos. 20 and 21 came from the Colorado and Southern Railroad, and Engines Nos. 22, 23 and 24 from the Silverton Northern, in 1943. All of these locomotives had been built by Baldwin in the late 1890s and early 1900s.

In 1943, 10 steam engines consigned to Iran were diverted to Skagway, converted from metered gauge to the three-foot gauge and used for the rest of the war. The engines, all 2-8-2s (a wheel alignment designation) built by Baldwin for the U.S. Army, were numbered 190 through 200. All were scrapped or sold after the war except No. 195, which is on display at the Trail of 98 Museum in Skagway.

Seven additional narrow-gauge engines built in 1923 by American Locomotive were purchased from the Denver, Rio Grande and Western Railroad in 1942 and used until 1945.

During the war the railroad accumulated 36 engines and almost 300 freight cars, some built for service in South America. More than 280,000 tons of material were carried to Whitehorse in 1943 — 45,000 tons in August alone. Thousands of troops and construction workers were also carried in both directions.

At the height of operations in 1943, dozens of trains rolled between Skagway and Whitehorse every day. As the war approached its end, the pressure eased, and none too soon. The railroad was literally worn out.

The 770th Railway Operating Battalion continued to run the railroad until control was returned to the prewar management on May 1, 1946.

Reprinted from a book by Stan Cohen

The White Pass railroad dock at Skagway, Alaska, was totally inadequate for the tons of material that were flowing into the port from the south for shipment on the railroad to Whitehorse, Yukon. USA SC322938 & SC323262

Officers in the 770th
Railway Operating Battalion
who operated the White Pass
and Yukon Route.
YA 85/78 #187

Headquarters and Supply
Battalion. YA 85/78 #170z

Roundhouse crew of the
770th Railway Operating
Battalion of Whitehorse,
Yukon. YA 85/78 #178

Loading material at the Skagway dock. In the background can be seen what is called the ships log—a rock formation in Skagway Harbor on which names of ships touching there have been painted, September 1942. SC 163094-B

Loading supplies into a boxcar for shipment to Whitehorse, Yukon. USA

The only highway crossing on the White Pass and Yukon Route just outside Whitehorse, on the Alcan Highway. USA SC323052

The steel cantilever bridge over Dead Horse Gulch was at one time the highest railroad bridge in the world. It has now been bypassed. YA 83/53

A train entering Skagway after a run to Whitehorse, December 1942. SC163120-B

Troops of the Railway
Operating Battalion at the
Skagway rail yard. DEDMAN'S
PHOTO SHOP SKAGWAY

Tracks were laid down Broadway in Skagway in 1898 and were removed to the edge of town after the war. The large
building in the center is the original 1900 railroad building, which is now the National Park Service Visitor's Center.
STAN COHEN COLLECTION

Snow was a huge problem in the White Pass. Here soldiers are repairing a rotary snowplow damaged by driving into heavy snow that was wet when it fell and froze with the tumbling temperatures to almost the consistency of concrete, 1944. USA SC200220

An engine flowing through a 16-foot snowbank on White Pass. Some of the worst weather in years occurred in the winter of 1942–43. SC283623

. . .

66

Soldiers shovel away snow from a derailed train. Three reels of cable en route to the ACS (Alaska Communications System) at Wildhorse, Yukon, for an airbase telephone system, rolled into the canyon and were never recovered, winter of 1944–45. SC247718

A train is snowed under on the railroad after a terrific snowstorm during the winter of 1944–45. SC7722

Frost covers the Whitehorse-Skagway telephone line amid deep snow in the winter of 1944–45. SC247714

Maj. John E. Auslund of Chicago, formerly with the Burlington Route, is shown talking to fireman, Pvt. Ross Weye of Havre, Montana. Auslund was the military superintendent of the railroad. SC163090-B

The rail yard at the upper end of Skagway, 1944.
NA 208-LU-4-7-2

Engine #195 pulling a train near Skagway, 1944. SC323064

Another troop train on the Great Northern Railway. The Great Northern, along with the Northern Pacific and the Chicago, Milwaukee, St. Paul and Pacific, acted as the channel for getting troops and supplies to the Alaska war area. RNE

Great Northern Railway tank cars on a mountain curve passing a set of M/W cars. RNE

This view on the Maine Central shows the cars used to transport wood pulp to the paper mills.
H.W. PONTIN PHOTO

. . .

69

Reading engines, surrounded by coal smoke, wait in the early morning for their daily drag runs. READING

SP 4176, a flat-nosed cab in the front of an articulated steam engine with a trainload of materials, was on the down-grade from Donner Summit heading for Oakland Port of Embarkation. These mammoths of the rails with their cab-in-front design hauled war material over one of the most strategic mountain passes in the country. Lines such as Donner never had a chance to cool off, having trains run over them 24 hours a day, seven days a week during the war years. RNE

Tank train on the grade just out of San Luis Obispo, Calif., on the SP's coast line. RNE

. . .

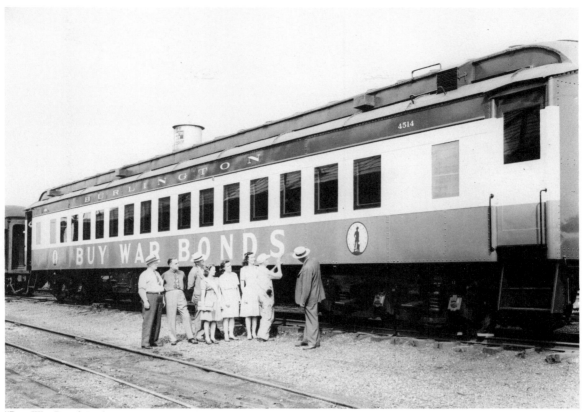

"Buy War Bonds" ad on the CB&Q Railroad's Burlington Route in August 1942. The car was painted red, white and blue. It looks like the painter, who was putting on the final touch at Aurora, Ill., had an appreciative audience.

The troops and civilian population still had to be fed. Here a trainload of Colorado sugar beets arrives at a factory in northern Colorado. US SUGAR BEET ASSOC.

Pre-war Budd Streamliners on the CBQ. These pioneer lightweight streamliners ran throughout the war years on the CBQ Midwest lines. CBQ

Boston & Maine's "Cheshire," another early lightweight streamliner, coming into the passenger platform. B&M RR

4
....

1943–1944:
Victories On All Fronts

*B*y January of 1943, the Allies were striking back on major fronts in Russia, North Africa, and in the South Pacific. At Stalingrad, the German armies were at least paying for the previous summer's lopsided advances into the south of Russia. The Soviets were rolling again, in the north as well as in the south, and in a way they never had before. The fantastic hope grew bright that they might cut off and destroy most of the 60 German divisions wallowing around in the Caucasus and the basins of the Don and Volga. The Russians had repenetrated the geographical boundary of the Ukraine, had surrounded the German armies pinned in Stalingrad, and had already recaptured most of the great bend of the Don.

Meanwhile, in Tunisia, the Allied armies ended months of stalemate and were on the offensive. The Americans, organized as a new Fifth Army under Lt. Gen. Mark Clark, held the respect of the cool British infantry: "They'll take anything and keep on punching. Those Yanks go in yelling and come out smiling. Between us, we'll lick the Huns."

The war in the Pacific was increasing. The tempo of air battles, inevitable preludes to new campaigns, picked up by January of 1943, leading to speculation that the U.S. was about to recapture the Solomons, Lae, Salamaua, and New Guinea. From Guadalcanal's Henderson Field, still littered with wrecked planes, Army and Navy bombers took off daily for the new Japanese base at Munda, bombing it heavily. The fight was on for full control of the South Pacific skies, everyone believing that who controlled the skies would determine the outcome of the war.

Back on the home front, the tempo on American rails had increased as well. During the year before when he was asked for a forecast of America's transportation prospects and problems in 1943, Joseph B. Eastman, director of the Office of Defense Transportation, said, "Looking ahead into 1943, I can make no other prediction than the same one I made a year ago, namely, that the remarkable transportation achievements of the past year must be excelled and that the job will be performed with increasing difficulty. Performed it will be, however, because it must."

And, of course, it was. Despite the mounting handicaps of manpower and equipment shortages, the nation's railroads in that year handled the greatest volume of freight and passenger traffic in the history of transportation. Freight trains rolled up the tremendous total of 725,000,000,000 revenue ton-miles, 14 percent above the figure for 1942, the previous record year. In 1943 alone, army freight and express was four and one-half times as great as during the entire period of World War I. Passenger traffic amounted to 85,000,000,000 passenger-miles, an increase of 58 percent over the high mark in 1942.

There was no question that 1943 had been an incredible year. American railroads had carried 72 percent of the burden of all freight transportation in the U.S. More intensive use was being made of available locomotives and cars, and inventories of unserviceable units had been reduced to all-time lows. Furthermore, over 255,000 skilled railroaders were now in the armed forces. In terms of taxes, the railroad tax bill in 1943 exceeded one billion, eight hundred and fifty million dollars, enough to pay and feed two and one-quarter million American soldiers for a full year. And, a number of sub-committees of the Association of American Railroads were studying every aspect of possible postwar problems.

By May of 1944, America was finishing a period

Flat cars with their loads on the wharf of an East Coast port of embarkation. Ship in the background is a Liberty Boat, which hauled the material brought down to the wharfs by the railroads.
USA

Erie Railroad #3387 hauling heavy steel invasion boats destined for the Navy on the East Coast. ERIE RAILROAD

A scene on the Lehigh Valley Railroad. A heavy tank is loaded onto a Nickel Plate Road flat for shipment to a port of embarkation.
LEHIGH VALLEY RR

· · ·

of four years of war-time achievements: one and a half years devoted to preparing, and two and a half years devoted to fighting. The nation's railways and shippers could review with great and patriotic pride what they had recently achieved. That astounding record should be told in great detail, lest we forget.

While again in 1944, the freight traffic being handled was the largest in history, it was increasing at a decelerating rate. Production for war purposes seemed to have about reached its final maximum. A few months before, it was estimated that only two-thirds as much of such production would be required to carry on the war against Japan, alone, as was now required to carry on the war against both Germany and Japan. Railways and shippers would have to continue to exert themselves to the utmost to keep available traffic moving the rest of 1944; but they could not begin giving real attention to the potential problems of transportation in the post-war period.

Anyone who had predicted four years before the enormous changes and increases in traffic demands upon the railways that had since occurred would have said the railways were entirely unprepared to meet them. New Deal "experts," who estimated much smaller increases in demands than had occurred, criticized railway management because it opposed a proposal for government to finance acquisition of 500,000 new freight cars. Soon afterward government restrictions began preventing the railways from getting anywhere near all the equipment and materials they actually ordered. And, in the year ended March 31,

1944, they rendered 122 percent more freight service than in the year ended March 31, 1940, with an increase of only 186,000, or 10 percent, in total freight cars on line and a small decrease in the number of road freight locomotives.

As pointed out several times, the nation's production had been enormously enlarged during the war by increasing manpower used in production, by huge investment in expansion of productive plant and by increased efficiency in the utilization of both manpower and plant. But there had been accomplished on the railways, with less manpower than was employed in the pre-depression years, with little expansion of plant during the war, and almost entirely because of enhanced efficiency, an increase in war-time freight service relatively greater than the increase in war-time production. And, in addition, the railways were handling a rapidly increasing passenger traffic that during the last year became four times as large as four years before.

Credit for what the railways had accomplished and were still accomplishing in handling freight had to be divided between them, their employees, the shippers, and the various government agencies. Without the cooperation of the shippers and government agencies the achievement would have been impossible. Also, it would have been entirely impossible without the many kinds of increases in efficiency that have been achieved by railway officers from the highest to the lowest, and the loyal support they have given to and gotten from their employees.

Four Years of Railroad Progress

	Twelve Months Ended			Per cent increase or decrease 1944 compared with	
	March 31, 1940	March 31, 1943	March 31, 1944	1940	1943
Investment in property (thous.)	$ 26,089,000	$ 26,643,405	$ 27,021,610	+ 3.6	+ 1.4
Revenue ton-miles (thous.)	333,767,510	676,843,679	738,642,302	+121.5	+ 9.1
Revenue passenger-miles (thous.)	23,135,375	62,701,267	92,683,414	+300.6	+47.8
Gross earnings (thous.)	4,083,596	8,073,747	9,236,567	+126.2	+14.4
Total operating expenses (inc. equip. and jt. facility rents) (thous.)	3,103,720	5,035,729	6,083,990	+ 96.0	+20.8
Taxes (thous.)	361,104	1,432,353	1,869,049	+417.6	+30.5
Net railway operating income (thous.)	618,100	1,603,933	1,283,527	+107.7	−20.0
Per cent earned on investment	2.37	6.02	4.75	+100.4	−21.0
Average number of employees	1,000,323	1,306,921	1,370,290	+ 37.0	+ 4.8
Equipment Situation	March 1, 1940	March 1, 1943	March 1, 1944		
Locomotives—					
Total number on line (inc. switching)	42,724	42,224	42,879	+ 0.4	+ 1.6
Number in bad order	9,562	4,440	4,807	− 49.7	+ 8.3
Number serviceable	33,162	37,784	38,072	+ 14.8	+ 0.8
Number stored serviceable (surplus)	3,058	667	633	− 79.3	− 5.0
Number in use	30,104	37,117	37,439	+ 24.4	+ 0.9
Road Freight Locomotives—					
Total number on line	22,478	22,035	22,341	− 0.6	+ 1.4
Number in bad order	5,760	2,620	2,808	− 51.3	+ 7.2
Number serviceable	16,718	19,415	19,533	+ 16.8	+ 0.6
Number stored serviceable (surplus)	1,817	297	307	− 83.1	+ 3.4
Number in use	14,901	19,118	19,226	+ 29.0	+ 0.6
Freight cars—					
Total number on line	1,852,690	2,026,092	2,038,796	+ 10.0	+ 0.6
Number in bad order	158,947	47,670	45,235	− 71.5	− 5.1
Number serviceable	1,693,743	1,978,422	1,993,561	+ 17.7	+ 0.8
Number surplus cars	177,873	41,130	17,351	− 90.2	−57.8
Number in use	1,515,870	1,937,292	1,976,210	+ 30.4	+ 2.0

· · ·

Man-Hours Worked—Railway Industry

Year	Maintenance of Way and Structures	Maintenance of Equipment and Stores	Train and Engine Service	All Occupations
	Aggregate			
1939	471,583,614	627,513,318	473,199,064	2,357,114,234
1940	491,070,269	624,886,199	508,671,576	2,478,712,804
1941	574,545,011	792,203,228	603,064,901	2,837,853,921
1942	659,347,324	892,321,450	724,035,585	3,248,983,846
1943	734,345,037	1,001,477,651	789,801,372	3,613,012,729
	Average Hours Per Employee Per Week			
1939	44.8	45.6	43.3	45.8
1940	45.2	46.0	44.1	46.2
1941	46.6	48.1	46.7	47.8
1942	48.0	48.8	49.3	49.0
1943	51.4	51.6	50.8	51.1

Average Hours Worked Per Employee Per Week—Other Industries

Year	Manufacturing Durables	Manufacturing Nondurables	Iron and Steel	Coal Mining Anthracite	Coal Mining Bituminous
1939	38.0	37.4	37.2	27.7	27.1
1940	39.3	37.0	38.6	27.2	28.1
1941	42.1	38.9	41.6	28.1	31.1
1942	45.0	40.0	42.8	33.8	32.7
1943	46.6	42.5	46.2	37.4	36.7

Railway, Present Employment and Additional Needs

Occupational group	Total Employment 3-15-44	Additional Needs 3-25-44 Number	Additional Needs 3-25-44 Per cent
Maintenance of way and structures	283,435	46,489	16.5
Maintenance of equipment and stores	391,000	29,557	7.6
Transportation—train and engine service	301,985	7,022	2.3
Transportation—other	182,162	8,804	4.8
Executives, officers, professional men, clerical and general help	241,066	2,489	1.0
Total	1,399,848	94,561	6.8

Train and Engine Service Statistics

Year	Road Train-Hours Freight	Road Train-Hours Passenger	Yard Switching Locomotive Hours Freight	Yard Switching Locomotive Hours Passenger
1939	27,117,916	11,052,978	36,657,621	3,210,253
1940	28,931,011	10,940,768	40,312,145	3,321,668
1941	34,442,752	11,097,794	48,759,756	3,492,429
1942	42,265,660	11,994,487	54,968,342	3,843,149
1943	45,449,335	13,350,310	57,467,367	4,374,435
1944 (a)	48,000,000	14,000,000	60,000,000	4,600,000

(a) Forecast

So, 1943–1944 witnessed the volume of freight traffic increasing. So did the number of new cars installed by the railroads, but not at the rate at which the demand was increasing. What prevented a breakdown of freight transportation under such conditions? The answer was an amazing increase in the fluidity of freight-car movement. That picture might best be presented by a comparison of performance in each of three months—January and October 1943 and January 1944.

With a revenue loading of nearly 3,100,000 cars in January 1943, 1,705,000 cars on line averaged 17.1 days between loadings. In January 1944, 1,714,000 cars moved nearly 3,400,000 car loads with 15.6 days per car between loadings. This difference of a day and a half between loadings was the equivalent of 145,000 cars, of which 54,500 were obtained by the reduction in the number of cars awaiting repairs and surplus, largely the latter, and over 91,000 cars by the expedited performance of the active cars. In October 1943, 1,718,000 cars handled about 3,900,000 revenue loadings, with an average of 13.8 car days between loadings. Comparing this with January 1944 there were still available the equivalent of 26,000 more cars than were utilized in January. All but about 4,000 of these were available as the result of expedited handling of the active cars; surpluses and cars under repairs were nearly as low in January as in October.

The outlook for additional new cars, while better than the year before, was by no means rosy and there seemed little likelihood of any marked relief from the shortages that had been continuous since the previous fall. The question had been raised whether the apparent car shortages were really not motive-power shortages. When the factors indicative of freight-car utilization continued to rise, there could be no general shortage of motive power. No doubt there had been sporadic local shortages, either of locomotives or crews, but mostly in the yard service. Certainly, both cars and locomotives continued to be worn out at a rate faster than the effects of wear and tear were being restored. Care had been exercised to insure safe operation, and deterioration of those kinds that could continue for considerable periods without causing a complete failure continued to accumulate.

A few words should be said about new developments in the signaling systems and how those systems helped to move freight during these critical years. Wartime transportation, involving large quantities of traffic that had to be moved promptly, had focused attention on the shortcoming of the out-moded system of authorizing train movements by timetable and train orders. The most important defect of this system of train direction was that trains lost too much time waiting on passing tracks, and in many instances waiting in yards after they were ready to go, when actually time and idle tracks were available to advance these trains. But this meant there had to be some means of authorizing them to do so on short notice, based on the minute-to-minute progress being made by other trains. This need was met with centralized traffic control, which included track circuit-controlled signals whereby the trains themselves automatically provided protection against collisions; power machines to operate passing track switches, thus saving train stops; and semi-automatic signals, the aspects of which authorized trains to move, thereby eliminating timetables and train orders.

Army motor tow launches at Washington's Potomac Yards on their way to European waters. USASC

Boston's South Hampton Street Yards. Note Naval aircraft carrier in background. The two New York, New Haven & Hartford diesel/electric switch engines worked this yard. NYNH&HRR

Of course, this system of C.T.C. was not new, but the results that were being accomplished in those territories in which it had been installed to help move war traffic was new. On many single track lines, the increased traffic resulted in serious delays under timetable and train order operation. Facing this fact, the railroads, the War Production Board, and the manufacturers coordinated in making it possible to extend C.T.C. so that since Dec. 7, 1942, centralized traffic control had been installed, or was under construction, on some 3,000 miles of line. The benefits of C.T.C. were that on the average every freight car saved approximately one minute on every mile of road so equipped. Thus, in one territory about 123 miles long, the average saving was two hours; and, on an engine district of 175 miles the saving was some three hours. These results were being accomplished without increasing the number of locomotives and in some instances the number was actually decreased.

Manpower Shortages in Key Mechanical Department Jobs*

Occupation	Apr. 1, 1944	March 1, 1944	June 29, 1943
Apprentices	1,032	1,173	1,263
Blacksmiths	177	160	127
Blacksmith helper	123	134	75
Boilermaker	1,186	1,058	491
Boilermaker helper	785	682	211
Car cleaner	604	582	261
Car man	3,088	2,558	1,721
Car man helper	1,690	1,552	543
Coach cleaner	697	508	619
Laborer shop	5,781	4,650	2,406
Machinist	3,842	3,451	2,219
Machinist helper	1,435	1,444	380
Painter	474	371	317
Patternmaker	20	19	6
Pipefitter	262	237	116
Sheetmetal worker	307	227	187
Upholsterer	75	55	37
Welder	145	124	43

* Figures compiled by the U. S. Railroad Retirement Board

Traffic to the West Coast
First 20 Days of April

	1943	1944
Trains held out of yards one hour or more	411	58
Trains delayed two hours or more for power	1,043	206
Trains delayed two hours or more for crews	96	59
Cars set out because of congestion*	68,424	0
Cars undelivered to connections because of inability to accept	2,999	64
Crews relieved because of the 16-hour law	347	37

* This represents a count of one car for each day the car was set out.

War bond drive at the CBQ Chicago general offices, February 1944. CBQ

Camp Kilmer, N.J. In foreground is a troop train with an Army kitchen car on the head-end. Other troop trains are being prepared in the background. USASC and AAR

Southern Pacific West Oakland Yards. Engines 1255 and 1269 await assignment at the east end of these important railroad yards. In the near background are the buildings of the large Oakland Naval Supply Center, while in the far background is the San Francisco-Oakland Bay Bridge. It was through these yards that the majority of war material passed through on the way to the Pacific war zone. RNE

In San Francisco, Calif., on an overcast day at the foot of Market Street in front of the world-famous Ferry Building we find State Belt Railroad of California little 0-6-0 #1 pulling a long troop train along the Embarcadero. RNE

Even the lowly gravel and sand train had its place in the war. Here is one of the SP's 2-8-0s hauling a sand train on what was once, years ago, the main line through San Francisco. This view in the Ocean View district, was taken in July 1943. Balboa High School is the large building to the right rear.
W.C. WHITAKER

. . .

City of San Francisco engine #SF-1 pulled this glamorous streamlined train between Oakland, Calif., and Chicago, Ill., over the SP-UP & CNW during the war years. This view shows the second generation "City" diesel/electric engine in 1941, shortly before the war, at the shops of the Interurban Electric Railway. These shops were later taken over by the General Engineering Co., as a shipyard. The city hall of Oakland, Calif., can be seen in the right background across the estuary. RNE

Another Oakland to Chicago train was the Forty Niner, not as fast or plush as the City of San Francisco. This view taken before the war shows the Forty Niner being hauled by one of the Union Pacific's few streamlined steam engines. UPRR

City of Denver No. CD-05. This first-generation diesel/electric streamliner was jointly owned by the UP & CNW for usage over trackage of these two trunk lines. This early train was painted UP Yellow and is shown leaving Denver in April 1942. CD-05 moved passengers during the war years, and lasted another eight years when she was scrapped in 1953. Note the high Rocky Mountains to the right rear beyond the city of Denver itself. UPRR

1944 Railway Operations

"Railroads of the United States underwent in 1944 the severest performance test of all time. They adequately and satisfactorily met the record-breaking demand for transportation service. In doing so, they again demonstrated their vital character as an arm of the military establishment, and made a highly important contribution to the welfare of the American people, both in respect to furtherance of the war effort, and in the satisfaction of civilian needs and requirements," said Dr. Julius H. Parmelee, Director, Bureau of Railway Economics, in January of 1945.

The war-time increases of both freight and passenger traffic continued in 1944, but at a reduced pace. After increasing during the first half of the year, freight traffic slightly declined during the second half. Consequently, revenue ton-miles of about 740 billion in 1944 handled by Class I railways were only about two percent larger than in 1943. Likewise, passenger traffic, after increasing in the first half of the year, gained little in the second half, and amounted to about 96 billion passenger-miles, or 10 percent more than in 1943. Total operating revenues of Class I railways were about $9,482 million, or about $427 million more than in 1943, as compared with an increase in 1943 of $1,600 million. The increase in operating expenses was about $731 million. Because operating expenses increased more than gross earnings, net operating income declined from $1,362 million in 1943 to about $1,095 million in 1944, and net income (after fixed charges) from $874 million to about $696 million. The railways continued to follow a very conservative policy regarding dividends, which, as in 1943, amounted to only about $216 million. After dividends in 1943, they carried about $657 million of net to surplus, and in 1944 only about $480 million.

What occurred on the railways during the war years is well indicated by the following graph, which shows the disposition made of their total receipts in 1929, 1942, 1943, and 1944. "Total receipts" include total operating revenues plus "other income." As the height of the pillars in the graph indicate, total receipts in 1942, 1943, and 1944 exceeded total receipts in 1929 by the following percentages: 1942, 15 percent; 1943, 39 percent; and 1944, 46 percent.

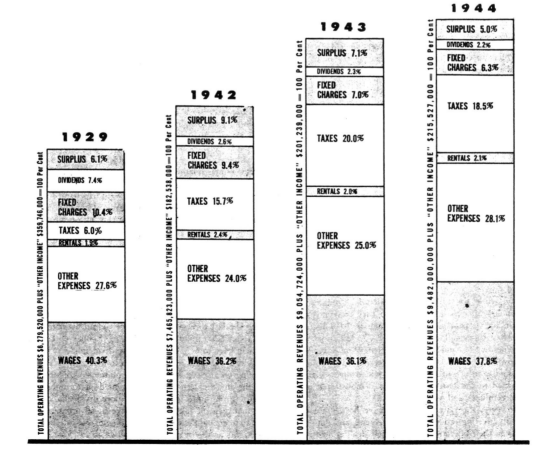

By the midpoint of 1944, American railroads found themselves in one of the most favorable positions with respect to motive power in their entire history. Naturally, the interpretation placed upon such a claim will depend almost entirely on the position of the reader in relation to the railroad industry, his knowledge of the motive power situation and his attitude toward it. The justification for the statement, according to H.C. Wilcox, associate editor of "Railway Age," lies in the fact that the carriers had many types of power to choose from, new types in prospect, and a wealth of operating experiences as a guide in formulating policies for the future.

In 1944, the traditional seasonal peaks that had characterized railroad operations disappeared in the rapidly mounting increases in traffic brought about by the war and had been replaced by a series of monthly records that stretched in an unbroken sequence from October 1944 to late 1944. Where before the war, the four-week October peak period required the use of 75 to 80 percent of the entire locomotive force in America, the carriers now were operating at a traffic rate requiring more than 85 percent of the locomotive inventory.

Spokane, Portland and Seattle #900 was the first of the Challenger-type 4-6-6-4s operated by this Columbia River line. Here shopmen work on her in 1945 at the Great Northern's Hillyard yards (seven miles out of Spokane). She's getting a little front-end attention as she has been placed on the ready track for movement down the Columbia River Route with heavy freight tonnage. H.W. PONTIN

Troop Trains

Soldiers on the move, who, according to an Army PR statement, "are never too tired to smile after their long cross-country train ride en route to the Staging Area." These troopers had just disembarked their pullmans on a train pulled by a Lehigh Valley Railroad steam engine at Camp Kilmer, N.J.
LEHIGH VALLEY RR

Nighttime at Chicago's Union Station. A detachment of WAACs, 46th Company, stand at attention before boarding their pullmans on April 10, 1943.
CBQRR

Women of the armed forces rode troop trains also. Here a group of nurses leaves Camp Kilmer en route to an embarkation center.
LEHIGH VALLEY RR

Here an old wooden baggage car was converted into a kitchen car. Pvt. C.S. Smith of the 87th Engineers is cutting meat on a kitchen car operating out of Fort Benning, Ga.
USA, 161 SIGNAL PHOTO CO.

Navy MPs stand outside of a passenger train at a rest stop somewhere on the CBQ RR line. CBQ RR

Bottom: There were not enough regular diner cars, so the Army designed this kitchen car for use on troop trains. This view, with civilian and Army officials, was taken at Aurora, Ill., on Oct. 9, 1943. USA

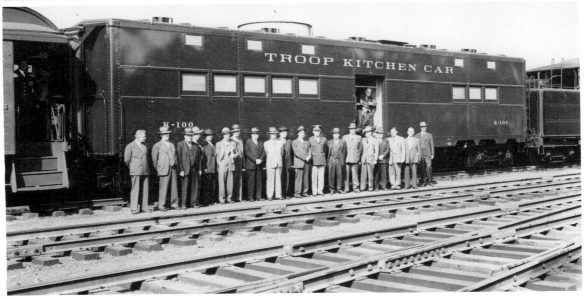

Union Pacific Railroad's Chicago Ticket Office Christmas Display, December 1943. UPRR

Union Pacific Railroad's Chicago labor recruiting display at UP ticket office, August 1945. The war had only a few days to go when this shot was snapped. UPRR

Pennsylvania RR 3548 — workhorse 2-8-0 — being turned around at the round-house ready for another full day of moving the freight.
RPS

SP's mountain climbers. No. 4294, war built cab-in-front mallet 4-8-8-2 sitting at Truckee, Calif., in June 1946. This engine is now at the California State RR Museum, Sacramento, Calif.
RNE

SP 4294 was the last articulated steam engine ordered by the Southern Pacific. This builder's view was taken at the Eddystone Shops of Baldwin Locomotive Works. Thanks to the Pacific Coast Chapter of the Railway Locomotive & Historical Society she was saved from the scrapper's torch. RNE

· · ·

"The Dixie Line" No. 550. This belle of the South was a mountain-type heavy dual-purpose locomotive that ran military trains across the hinterlands of Tennessee. After the war the NC&StL was absorbed into the Louisville and Nashville system. L&N

Chicago & Eastern Illinois No. 1000. This mid-continent railroad was one of the major north-south railroads that operated out of Chicago to Evansville, Ill. During the war years it was a busy line. Engines like the 1000 pulled the varnish at high speed across the farmlands of Illinois. RNE

Even the camelbacks did their share. Here is Reading's 346, 4-4-2 high-stepping camelback (where the cab is placed in front of the enlarged boiler—which was needed because the engines burned soft coal). RNE

The Diesel-Electric Locomotive: Making Railroad Utilization More Known

*F*ortunately, many railroads had prepared themselves for the coming of war by the purchases (over a period of five to ten years) of modern high-capacity steam units and the adoption of the diesel-electric locomotive in both road and switching service. The operating advantages of the diesel-electric are well known and it is sufficient to say that the records it established during the first three years of war have brought home to railroad managements the value of, and the possibilities in, intensive utilization of power. The diesel-electric provided competition that had acted, like the electric locomotive some 20 years before, as a challenge to steam. Its outstanding performance in selected cases of traffic had developed within railroad operating and mechanical organizations both the necessity and the desire to find out whether or not steam power could approach these performances. The same challenge had also been responsible, together with many technological developments, as a result of the war, for a renewed interest in experimentation with several new types, such as the steam-turbine and the gas-turbine locomotives.

All of these factors combined to create a situation wherein the railroads were occupying, whether safely so or not, a grandstand seat at one of the world's greatest transportation performances and, viewing as they could, the men and the machines with which this act had been assembled, felt reasonably sure that they were justified in waiting to see what would happen next. In essence, this was just another way of saying that they were at the moment in the position of having done an excellent job with the tools at hand and were waiting to see what direction the developments of the immediate future would take before embarking upon an extensive program of equipment replacement.

According to Wilcox in an article entitled "Locomotives—What Kind and Why?", which appeared in "Railway Age" on Jan. 6, 1945, the operating department of a railroad formed its judgment of motive power from such factors as availability and failure-free performance in service. Being the custodian of gross ton-miles, it knew that the locomotive that could spend the greatest number of hours per day out on the road in revenue service would be the cheapest, on a ton-mile basis, in the long run. It was not necessarily concerned with matters of design, or in any thing not directly related to the utilization of locomotives. In short, that department did not care how or where the mechanical departments got the locomotives that it produced upon call just so long as they were there when needed and did the job they were called upon to perform. An appreciation of this fact will help to understand why the diesel has been so popular with the operating man and why it has been called the "answer to an operating man's prayer." It came into the railroad picture at a time and under conditions that have not only made it possible

The streamlined engine of the New York Central Railroad's Commodore Vanderbilt train. RPS

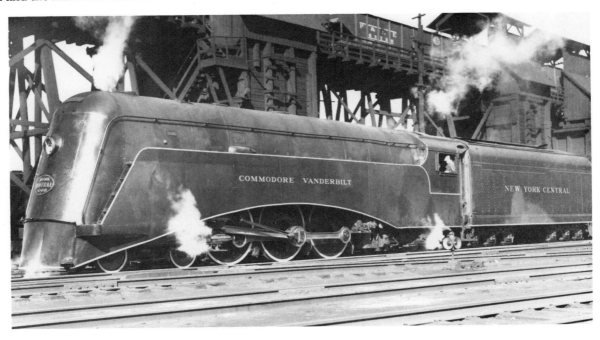

for it to demonstrate its abilities and economy on a ton-mile basis in its own right, but served to set a pace for other types of power that had brought out hidden values and possibilities not realized before. The impetus of that pacesetting was largely responsible for the operating performances that placed the railroads in 1945 in a position of confidence born of accomplishment. It also placed them in a position in which there was danger—and opportunity.

The war was not going to last forever. When it did end, the railroads would again be faced with the problem of conducting business in a world of intense competition in the field of transportation and where success or failure would depend entirely upon the ability to meet that competition on a profitable basis. Experience had shown those whose responsibility was to acquire and operate motive power was the volume and the spacing of traffic loads. Possibly there never had been a time in railroad history when management was so greatly in need of a coldly practical appraisal of the entire motive-power question. The operating department, experienced as it was in the costs of operation and the problems connected with them, was qualified to speak with authority within the realm of its function and experience. But, of course, management had every right to look to the mechanical department for the answers to questions concerning design, maintenance, and type of motive power. In early 1945, management had to also look to someone for the answers to questions relating to the economics of the motive-power problem and on all too many roads found itself in the position of being obliged to get answers from the operating departments that really should have come from the mechanical departments.

And, of course, management was also faced with the necessity of apportioning expenditures for improvements between motive power and rolling stock, roadway improvements, shop and terminal improvements and a myriad of other opportunities for worthwhile investment. The largest items in the entire category of railroad expenditures was locomotive repairs and locomotive fuel. The proponents of diesel power not only claimed that it would save the railroad millions of dollars in these two expense items alone, but that it was an operating facility with none of the disadvantages of steam power. Those who backed the steam locomotive claimed that, if given the same chance, it would do just as good a job as the diesel and do it cheaper besides. Here were two sides of the motive-power battle in the opening months of 1945: a battle in which the steam locomotive was not holding its ground too well. The contestants in that battle were not only steam versus the diesel locomotive, but the operating versus the mechanical department. Railroad management stood as the referee and in most cases had already recognized that there were intangible factors involved in the problem that it might well further investigate before announcing any decision. Wilcox commented, "Unfortunately, from the railroad standpoint, motive power and its operation involved such tremendous expenditures that every hour and day in which obsolete facilities are continued in service the roads are spending—or possibly throwing away—the dollars that would help pay for their future success."

DRGW #540. New diesel-electric locomotive placed in service in 1942. She helped this trans-Rocky Mountain railroad handle the military shipments in both directions. DRGWRR

Santa Fe 2301, with a 600 hp. ALCO/GE diesel/electric switch engine, was in operation at the Calwa Yards, south of Fresno, Calif., in November 1944. ATSF

This old oil/electric engine No. 1000 was one of the first engines of its type. Here she is working the yards of the Jersey Central after the war years. JC LINES

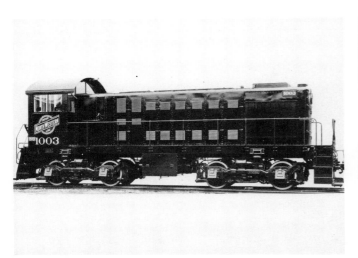

CNW No. 1003 was brand new when this photo was taken in May 1942. A 1000 hp. diesel switching engine built by the American Locomotive Works, she was a welcome addition to an already overburdened wartime railroad. AMERICAN LOCOMOTIVE CO.

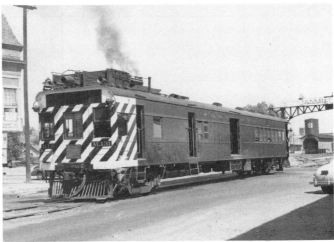

Motor passenger rail car No. M-131. Sunny day in July 1942, seven months after Pearl Harbor she sits idly waiting to start her run from Fresno, Calif., down the San Joaquin Valley to Visalia, Porterville, Terra Bella and Tulare. Those were the years that anything and everything that could run was placed in use. These hardy motor rail cars certainly filled in the gap on the branch lines. ATSF RAILWAY

Is Your Trip Essential?

Herb Roth in the Delray Beach News (used by permission)

COMPARING 1944 WITH PRE-WAR:	
	Percent
Revenue ton-miles increased	153.4
Tons handled increased	114.5
Export freight increased	223.2
Average load per car increased	7.9
Train speed increased over 1943	1.9
Miles per car per day increased	54.5
Freight car ownership *decreased*	25.0
New cars installed *decreased*	56.3
Surplus cars *decreased*	87.1
Cars over 25 years old	30.7

Purchases of Equipment, Materials and Fuel
By All Class I Railroads in 1943 and 1944

	1944* (000)	1943 (000)	Increase Per Cent
Equipment**	$255,000	$248,000	3
Rail	73,779	60,074	23
Crossties	91,065	83,402	9
All Other Material..	882,710	723,509	22
Total from Manufacturers	$1,302,554	$1,114,985	17
Fuel	589,326	527,296	12
Grand Total	$1,891,880	$1,642,281	15

* Preliminary estimates by Railway Age.
** Equipment figures are for amount *delivered* in 1943 and for amount *ordered* in 1944.
Total railway purchases of all durable goods from manufacturers charged to both capital and operation were larger in both years than the figures given in the table.

Age of Freight-Carrying Cars on Class I Railroads as of January 1, 1944

Years old	Number of cars	Per cent of total*
1 to 5	243,301	13.85
6 to 10	151,997	8.65
11 to 15	157,663	8.98
16 to 20	365,106	20.79
21 to 25	299,238	17.03
Over 25	539,329	30.7

* Total ownership 1,756,634.

. . .

Table I—Comparative Traffic Statistics

REVENUE CARLOADINGS
(thousands

1944.......	43,500	1939.......	33,911
1943.......	42,440	1933.......	29,220
1942.......	42,826	1929.......	52,828
1941.......	42,290	1923.......	49,812
1940.......	36,358	1918.......	44,592

REVENUE TON-MILES
(millions)

1944.......	740,000	1939.......	333,438
1943.......	727,075	1933.......	249,223
1942.......	637,,983	1929.......	447,322
1941.......	475,072	1923.......	412,727
1940.......	373,253	1918.......	405,379

REVENUE PASSENGER-MILES
(millions)

1944.......	96,000	1939.......	22,651
1943.......	87,820	1933.......	16,341
1942.......	53,659	1929.......	31,074
1941.......	29,350	1923.......	37,957
1940.......	23,762	1920.......	46,849
		1918.......	42,677

Annual Purchases of Materials and Supplies
Class I Railroads
(Equipment Excluded)

	Fuel (000)	Rail (000)	Cross Ties (000)	Other Material (000)	Total (000)	Total Less Fuel (000)
1929	$336,805	$88,735	$143,874	$759,186	$1,328,600	$991,795
1930	308,277	60,980	127,652	538,591	1,035,500	727,223
1931	244,500	41,500	44,000	365,000	695,000	450,500
1932	178,250	15,500	27,550	223,700	445,000	266,750
1933	179,150	10,650	19,750	248,200	457,750	278,600
1934	220,000	33,200	39,700	332,100	625,000	405,000
1935	232,400	20,354	33,780	306,593	593,127	360,727
1936	271,398	37,237	41,360	452,309	802,304	530,906
1937	293,540	44,935	58,361	562,100	958,936	665,396
1938	243,889	23,920	37,911	277,091	582,811	338,922
1939	257,880	38,340	39,760	434,394	770,374	512,494
1940	273,677	45,418	47,995	488,883	855,973	582,296
1941	349,848	52,311	50,039	710,831	1,163,029	813,181
1942	426,335	55,647	63,153	714,676	1,259,811	833,476
1943	527,296	60,074	83,402	723,509	1,394,281	866,985
1944*	589,326	73,779	91,065	882,710	1,636,880	1,047,554

* Preliminary Estimates.

Selected Operating Statistics
First ten months 1944-1943

	1944	1943	Inc. or Dec.	% Change
Freight train-kms.	13,858,988	14,559,321	700,333	4.8
Passenger train-kms.	7,712,200	8,738,099	1,025,899	11.7
Mixed and spec. train-kms.	3,805,371	3,167,787	637,584	20.1
Non-revenue train-kms. ...	319,886	172,650	147,236	85.3
Total train-kms.	25,696,445	26,637,857	941,412	3.5
Passenger car kms.	76,654,576	73,767,379	2,887,197	3.9
Frt. loaded car kms.	221,083,842	228,123,121	7,039,279	3.1
Frt. empty cars kms.	87,531,074	92,679,044	5,147,970	.5.6
Total frt. car kms.	308,614,916	320,802,165	12,287,249	3.8
Net ton-kms. (1000s)	6,657,878	6,416,459	241,419	3.8
Gross ton-kms. (1000s)	14,227,663	14,115,852	111,811	0.8
Total No. cars loaded	414,090	424,999	10,909	2.6

Averages

	1944	1943	Inc. or Dec.	% Change
Net ton-kms. per train-km.	446	421	25	5.9
Gross ton-kms. per train-km.	903	884	19	2.1
Speed per hr. (kms.) Ft. ..	18.2	20.1	1.9	9.5
Gross ton-kms. per train hr.	16,463	17,793	1,330	1.1
Frt. loc. kms. daily	167	178	11	6.2
Liters oil per 1000 GTK-frt.	47.5	43.2	4.3	10.0
% loaded car-kms. to total..	71.6	71.1	0.5	0.7
Net tons per car	30.1	28.1	2.0	3.3
Kms. line operated	11,740	11,757	17	0.1

Table I—Freight Cars Ordered for Domestic Service in 1944

Builder	Railroads	Industrial and Private Car Cos.	Total	Per Cent of Total
Company Shops	10,844	400	11,244	24
Contract Car Builders	33,981	1,708	35,689	76
Total	44,825	2,108	46,933	100

Note.—Orders by U. S. Government departments are excluded.

Table II—Domestic Car Orders by Type and Purchaser

Type of Freight Car Ordered	Railroads 1944	Railroads 1943	Industrial and Private Car Cos. 1944	Industrial and Private Car Cos. 1943	Total Orders 1944	Total Orders 1943
Box	23,860	8,853	56	2	23,916	8,855
Hopper	12,695	18,675	31	25	12,726	18,700
Gondola	7,224	8,940	135	214	7,359	9,154
Flat	550	2,577	72	88	622	2,665
Tank	....	50	326	516	326	566
Refrigerator	3	....	1,412	....	1,415	....
Air-Dump	137	4	70	113	207	117
Caboose	56	437	....	....	56	437
Miscellaneous	300	47	6	....	306	47
Total	44,825	39,583	2,108	958	46,933	40,541

Note.—1943 totals are adjusted to eliminate orders subsequently cancelled in 1944 due to WPB restrictions on building.

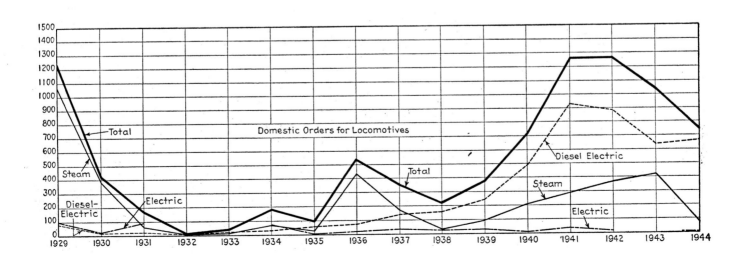

Table I—Passenger-Train Cars Ordered, 1929-1944

Year	Domestic	U. S. Export	Total U. S.	Canadian
1944	540	..	540	..
1943	70	..	70	..
1942	2	..	2	..
1941	497	19	516	72
1940	389	21	410	65
1939	320	28	348	87*
1938	274	..	274	24
1937	679	..	679	99
1936	425	..	425	10
1935	95	..	95	16
1934	388	15	403	..
1933	6	..	6	..
1932	39	..	39	..
1931	11	21	33	11
1930	648	15	663	203
1929	2,322	33	2,355	122

Note.—The totals of domestic and U. S. export orders for years 1941-1944 exclude U. S. Government purchases. Domestic orders placed in 1941-1943 are adjusted to eliminate orders subsequently cancelled due to WPB restrictions on building. In certain instances domestic orders placed in December are not reported until following year; statistics for years 1929-1943 are adjusted to eliminate this overlap.

Table II—Passenger-Train Cars Built, 1929-1944

Year	Domestic	U. S. Export	Total U. S.	Canadian
1944	...	...	...	...
1943	...	21	21	..
1942	242	11	253	40
1941	299	8	307	32
1940	142	28	170	30
1939	194	..	194	27*
1938	264	..	264	38
1937	664	..	664	70
1936	142	..	142	10
1935	197	..	197	..
1934	268	15	283	..
1933	6	..	6	..
1932	39	..	39	..
1931	198	21	219	66
1930	1,264	40	1,304	210
1929	1,254	20	1,274	162

* Includes export deliveries.
Note.—Passenger-train cars built for the U. S. Government and for lend-lease not reported in 1942-1944.

Table I—Locomotives Ordered, 1929-1944

	Domestic				U. S. Export	Canadian (Inc. Export)
Year	Steam	Diesel	Electric	Total		
1944	74	670	3	747	134	324
1943	413	635	..	1,048	60	241
1942	363	894	12	1,269	32	53
1941	293	937	38	1,268	85	79
1940	207	492	13	712	85	3
1939	119	249	32	400	40	56
1938	36	160	29	225	24	35
1937	173	145	36	354	56	57
1936	435	77	24	536	22	1
1935	30	60	7	97	15	27
1934	72	37	76	185	17	..
1933	17	25	..	42	7	i
1932	5	7	..	12	1	i
1931	62	21	91	174	28	2
1930	382	18	21	421	20	95
1929	1,055	80	95	1,230	106	77

Note:—The totals of domestic and U. S. export orders for years 1941-1944, exclude U. S. Government purchases. Domestic orders placed in 1941-1943 are adjusted to eliminate orders subsequently cancelled due to W.P.B. restrictions on building. In certain instances, domestic orders placed in December are not reported until following year; statistics for years 1929-1943 are adjusted to eliminate this overlap.

Table II—Domestic Diesel Locomotive Orders by Horsepower and Purchaser

Horsepower	Railroads 1944	1943	Industrial Cos. and Private Car Lines 1944	1943	Total 1944	1943
6,000	6	3	..	..	6	3
5,400	39	70	..	..	39	70
4,050	8	..	..	..	8	..
4,000	22	38	..	..	22	38
2,700	8	..	..	..	8	..
2,000	78	22	..	..	78	22
1,350	18	..	..	..	18	..
1,000	334	342	..	11	334	353
660-600	57	31	23	6	80	37
Less than 600	26	30	51	82	77	112
Total	596	536	74	99	670	635

Note:—1943 totals are adjusted to eliminate orders subsequently cancelled in 1944.

Table III—Locomotives Built, 1929-1944

Year	Domestic	U. S. Export	Total U. S.	Canadian
1944	1,171	78	1,249	189
1943	1,012	58	1,070	94
1942	936	11	947	71
1941	1,047	57	1,104	3
1940	435	66	501	59
1939	338	16	354	1
1938	272	28	300	46
1937	526	44	570	45
1936	157	22	179	23
1935	184	17	201	4
1934	91	19	110	..
1933	57	6	63	..
1932	102	18	120	3
1931	181	17	198	24
1930	972	51	1,023	111
1929	926	139	1,065	96

Note:—Domestic and U. S. export totals for 1942-1944 exclude locomotives built for the U. S. Government and lend-lease.

Miles of Main Track Built in the United States in 1944

State	Number of companies building	First track	Second track	Third track	Fourth track	Total
Alaska	1	12.40	....	...	....	12.40
Florida	1	7.00	....	....	....	7.00
Georgia	1	2.43	....	....	....	2.43
Illinois	2	0.60	1.96	....	....	2.56
Iowa	1	1.81	....	....	....	1.81
Kentucky	3	31.81	7.70	....	....	39.51
Maine	1	....	10.60	....	....	10.60
Maryland	1	....	....	8.85	....	8.85
Missouri	1	....	1.87	....	....	1.87
Montana	1	....	9.86	....	....	9.86
New Mexico	1	....	1.25	....	....	1.25
North Carolina	2	15.30	4.85	....	....	20.15
North Dakota	1	....	13.00	....	....	13.00
Ohio	1	....	1.14	0.08	0.23	1.45
Oklahoma	1	7.15	....	....	....	7.15
Pennsylvania	2	1.18	0.82	6.14	....	8.14
South Dakota	1	....	0.93	....	....	0.93
Texas	1	8.82	....	....	....	8.82
Utah	1	....	7.26	....	....	7.26
Washington	1	12.67	....	....	....	12.67
West Virginia	2	16.82	....	....	....	16.82
Wyoming	1	3.08	....	....	....	3.08
Total		121.07	61.24	15.07	0.23	197.61

The Military Railway Services Drives Toward Berlin

*B*y the end of 1944, the Army Transportation Corps had procured and shipped overseas some 4,000 American-built locomotives and 60,000 freight cars. Its personnel was active in every theater of land operations in the world-wide conflict. In its 1944 overseas performance, the Military Railway Service had abundantly proven the value of its months of preparation for the job of keeping the supply lines open and materials of war moving forward to meet demands all along the battlefront. Within four months after the port of Cherbourg was available, some 20,000 freight cars and 1,300 locomotives had been moved across the English Channel, in addition to 37 hospital trains and various specialized railway equipment. Much of this was American-built, shipped across the Atlantic more or less knocked-down for assembly by M.R.S. units in England. The rest was British railway equipment adapted for military use in France. In addition, as rapidly as French territory was given up by the retreating Germans, additional rolling stock which they left behind became available for M.R.S. use. All property belonging to railroads taken over in whole or in part by M.R.S. personnel in France was being utilized to capacity, and capacity was being measured in terms of war necessity and American operating methods, as far as they were applicable under the prevailing physical and military conditions.

Plans had been developed well in advance to bring over regular railway equipment as soon as the boats could get into Cherbourg Harbor. The available train-ferry vessels were those that had been used in pre-war days to shuttle the London-Paris trains across the Channel. These boats were so few, and their capacity was so limited, that it was estimated that three and one-half years would have been required to ferry over with them the rail equipment that would be needed to support the advance of the fighting front.

Faced with this limitation, the committee set up an arrangement by which the pre-war train ferries were assigned to the job of carrying locomotives, while a number of ships of the LST-2 type were converted to car ferries. Three parallel tracks, connected with switches, were laid on the flat lower deck of these tank carriers, giving each a capacity of 22 freight cars. The next problem was that of overcoming a 24-foot rise and fall of the tide on the French shore which would have limited landing operations through fixed facilities to some one and a half hours at each high tide. This was met by constructing a long, jointed, wheeled bridge that rested on a railway track sloping into the water and which in turn carried a standard-gauge railway track. This contraption was pushed in and pulled out by the action of the tide, maintaining a continuous connection with the permanent track through sleeves fitted over the head of each rail. An apron afforded a connection with the open mouth of the LST, enabling the vessel's load of cars to be run ashore without delay at any hour.

Steam-powered 0-6-0 switchers and 2-8-0 road locomotives formed the bulk of the train ferries' contribution to the trans-Channel movement. However, in addition to the 150-hp. diesels brought in over the beaches, and others of this and larger sizes that were assigned to switching service, some 130 road diesels of the 650-hp. type and 26 of the 380-hp. type were soon put ashore in France. The diesels were particularly useful near the fighting lines, as the lack of smoke and steam plumes made them much less conspicuous targets than steam-powered units for enemy fliers and artillerists, while their ability to make long runs without stops for fuel and water was a further advantage in operating on lines where rehabilitation of such supplementary facilities had not been completed.

Because bombings played havoc on the French rails (France's pre-war supply of 18,500 locomotives, 515,000 freight cars, and 31,100 passenger cars were virtually all destroyed), relief for the Allied Armies had to come via Antwerp. The Belgian lines were under joint British and American military control and served as a most useful series of lines for the British armies concentrated in the northern sector of the Allied advance. Antwerp's pre-war facilities, relatively undamaged and able to handle some 40,000 tons of freight daily, were relieving the burden on the French ports. The purpose of the Battle of the Bulge was to recapture Antwerp because Hitler realized how much freight was pouring through that port. Antwerp's pre-war freight volume was around 3,000 tons a month. Within three weeks of its recapture by the Allied armies, it was handling 20,000 tons or more a day. Supplies were going forward on Belgian railroads in volume that required the operation of forty-one 400-ton freight trains daily. For a while, diesel-powered trains were run through from Antwerp to the front line supply bases, but it was found preferable to use these shorter units, designed primarily for switching, in shorter runs near the front, using steam power for the faster long runs.

Altogether, the Allied armies took over five main lines in France, as well as considerable secondary trackage. About 1,500 miles of railroad was rehabilitated and large new yards were created to take care of the unprecedented traffic. In order to make full use of the French signaling installations and station facilities, the plan to make right-hand operation on double-track lines standard practice for M.R.S. operations was changed after some experiments to the left-hand method prevailing in France. Where trains passed into areas using right-hand operation as standard practice, such as in Germany, that method was used since pre-war installations of crossovers and other facilities were generally adapted to this procedure.

In Italy, 2,478 miles of railroad had been repaired by the end of 1944. During that year, 21,759 trains had carried over seven million tons of military freight to Allied armies fighting their way up the Italian peninsulas. This figure did not include 3,154 troop trains and 812 hospital trains, which were also run. That traffic was handled largely with repaired Italian equipment, including 785 steam and electric locomotives and 28,127 cars, which were rehabilitated by Allied troops.

However, some 225 American-built locomotives and 200 freight cars were brought in to supplement the equipment taken over. Brig. Gen. Carl R. Gray Jr., commander of the M.R.S. troops in Italy, reported that his railway soldiers, following the advance of the line of battle and often working within range of enemy artillery, built over 14,900 feet of new bridging, rebuilt 24 tunnels with a total length of 20 miles, and moved half a million cubic yards of earth to fill gaps in viaduct and craters left by explosions. Over 750 miles of signal lines were also restored and 170 miles of new railway lines constructed.

As 1944 ended, the M.R.S. was looking forward to the day when it would be called upon to operate railroads leading directly to Berlin. In the words of Brig. Gen. Andrew F. McIntyre, chief of the Rail Division, Office of the Chief of Transportation, "No one is yet sure as to the requirements of the future, but whatever demands may be made upon the armies of the United States, you will find Military Railway Service troops right up there close behind the battle lines doing their parts."

Table 3—September, 1945, Troop Movements and Equipment Furnished by Carriers

Date	Travel Time 12 hrs. to 23 inc. Personnel		Travel Time 24 hrs. to 35 inc. Personnel		Travel Time 36 hrs. to 47 inc. Personnel		Travel Time 48 hrs. to over Personnel	
	Coaches	Sleeping Cars	Coaches	Sleeping Cars	Coaches	Sleeping Cars	Coaches	Sleeping Cars
Sept. 1	5,795	689	7,390	1,438	3,350	4,153	834	9,079
2	3,018	749	729	1,338	776	2,019	125	2,982
3	7,873	697	5,306	1,114	3,539	2,456	178	7,193
4	7,425	2,085	5,490	2,177	1,380	3,556	....	4,866
5	4,675	2,518	3,219	3,510	796	3,802	443	5,915
6	3,967	932	618	3,876	354	4,852	102	2,965
7	6,767	1,301	4,155	4,079	1,851	4,441	....	6,713
8	5,045	2,295	2,790	2,514	2,130	4,077	21	6,362
9	3,732	1,470	520	2,438	2,520	1,971	....	3,842
10	3,604	1,574	2,246	4,113	753	3,465	177	5,255
11	9,430	3,282	6,362	6,108	2,567	5,398	139	10,335
12	9,906	4,647	4,163	3,188	1,476	2,738	467	6,546
13	4,585	4,475	2,553	2,777	123	4,214	466	6,127
14	6,157	3,523	3,679	4,845	1,923	2,714	200	9,021
15	5,422	1,176	4,012	3,994	1,499	3,876	....	11,004
16	8,531	1,039	5,075	1,697	702	3,054	497	7,144
17	6,646	822	6,020	2,422	1,009	2,895	551	9,814
18	9,333	1,811	8,364	1,995	1,015	3,561	1,404	6,011
19	4,866	1,442	3,261	3,665	1,432	1,738	1,719	3,761
20	11,486	1,670	6,409	3,421	2,309	2,420	2,335	12,071
21	10,381	1,308	5,856	1,438	3,683	3,583	1,285	12,753
22	6,890	2,528	5,407	3,257	1,706	3,452	....	12,268
23	3,377	547	1,956	1,726	381	1,241	....	2,158
24	3,735	1,148	2,518	3,618	540	2,411	120	5,489
25	4,671	991	1,335	2,131	110	1,965	....	11,154
26	3,792	1,191	2,106	2,049	1,254	376	....	7,630
27	3,435	4,146	884	2,164	1,712	2,364	....	8,529
28	6,271	1,939	2,642	2,525	1,741	1,514	....	8,150
29	4,573	1,832	809	3,714	94	2,089	124	6,225
30	5,282	1,365	1,413	5,606	·103	1,396	600	3,691
Total	180,670	55,192	107,287	88,937	42,828	87,786	11,787	215,053
	76.600%	23.400%	54.675%	45.325%	32.789%	67,211%	5.196%	94.804%

Troop train meets troop transports at Newport, Va.
Typical embarkation scene taken during World War II at
Hampton Roads Port of Embarkation showing naval
transports #67 and #77 on north side of Pier #2 Newport
News. The coaches from which the troops are unloading
look quite old, most likely pre-World War I vintage. AAR

Table 1—Military Personnel Handled in Organized Movements

Year and Month	Number of Movements		Number of Cars	Passengers Carried	Passenger Miles (Thousands)
1942	(On Regular Trains)	(Special Trains)			
March	845	1,183	15,762	406,859	451,808
April	991	1,459	19,364	517,311	589,093
May	1,161	1,361	18,283	494,678	550,295
June	1,400	1,385	20,908	485,766	524,840
July	1,703	1,684	25,787	600,145	670,376
August	2,042	1,893	28,391	714,492	804,150
September	3,024	2,496	34,068	875,420	1,015,939
October	3,304	2,445	31,577	887,054	997,106
November	3,092	2,898	36,276	973,246	1,120,933
December	3,075	2,444	27,662	857,836	962,481
1943					
January	3,554	2,739	34,904	953,458	1,100,664
February	3,905	2,595	27,895	904,086	1,015,000
March	4,141	3,203	36,522	1,099,457	1,309,323
April	4,216	3,023	38,545	1,098,395	1,209,535
May	4,031	2,184	29,915	881,816	925,122
June	4,040	2,471	37,399	983,797	1,062,717
July	4,038	2,410	29,769	935,806	1,027,848
August	3,884	2,766	36,569	1,104,426	1,291,849
September	3,653	2,605	35,844	1,027,663	1,215,253
October	3,391	2,339	28,277	882,249	952,716
November	3,346	2,373	30,827	901,204	984,673
December	3,011	2,507	29,049	859,099	932,114
1944					
January	3,170	2,489	31,314	888,416	1,034,033
February	3,023	2,613	29,718	908,550	971,334
March	3,433	2,924	35,426	1,084,589	1,242,167
April	3,318	3,214	34,008	1,070,810	1,201,963
May	2,858	2,277	27,028	848,953	831,842
June	2,615	2,349	26,557	815,726	814,087
July	2,812	2,180	26,075	778,216	870,923
August	2,880	2,558	27,540	838,551	904,517
September	2,901	2,784	30,109	920,370	1,088,956
October	2,644	2,797	27,779	869,297	1,002,912
November	2,683	2,723	24,660	756,692	842,806
December	2,689	2,987	24,311	761,178	845,027
1945					
January	2,756	2,902	23,286	727,650	807,860
February	2,374	2,714	20,860	641,981	740,480
March	2,455	3,220	20,387	637,890	644,009
April	2,244	2,778	18,740	594,672	622,246
May	2,631	3,305	21,622	684,007	819,174
June	3,224	4,240	25,795	909,924	962,289
July	3,467	4,468	27,979	1,032,758	1,097,040
August	3,659	4,779	35,166	1,266,210	1,399,307

Table 2—Military Personnel Handled in Organized Movements

August, 1945

Branch of Service	Type of Move		Total Passengers
	Regular Trains Passengers	Special Trains Passengers	
Army	145,743	956,511	1,102,254
Patients	13,783	27,757	41,540
Prisoners of war	2,339	29,958	32,297
Navy	24,581	44,576	69,157
Marine	2,036	11,205	13,241
Coast Guard	3,409	335	3,744
Miscellaneous	2,161	1,816	3,977
Total passengers	194,052	1,072,158	1,266,210
Passenger-miles (Thousands)	189,783	1,209,524	1,399,307

Type of Equipment	Cars	Cars	Cars
Sleeper	3,546	12,582	16,128
Coach	1,797	10,561	12,358
Baggage	222	2,115	2,337
Kitchen	237	2,370	2,607
Hospital	939	766	1,705
Freight	8	23	31
Total cars	6,749	28,417	35,166

792

5
....

Final Victory: Great Days Ahead for America's Railroads

With Hitler's suicide in his bunker below the gutters of Berlin, and with the dropping of two atomic bombs on Japanese cities, World War II came to an end. It had been the most tragic and costly war in the history of man and its after-effects would be felt for several more decades. However, Americans would be justly proud of their railroads and the men and women running them. They had performed miracles in war-time transportation. Thanks to them, America was able to fabricate ships hundreds of miles from sea coasts, to build the world's largest navy, to create the greatest airpower, and to transport eleven million citizens to and from training camps, as well as to equip, feed, and maintain them.

The biggest transportation job in all history had a major hand in bringing about victory. And, America's railroads had carried these loads in spite of shortages of manpower and equipment. At the same time, they did a magnificent job of serving the home front. This unconquerable spirit of the nation's railroad men and women assured new achievements in transportation. Greater comfort, safety, and convenience would be offered travelers. Faster freight schedules would enable shippers to get goods to markets quicker and fresher.

There was no question about it. There would be great days ahead for America's railroads. The carriers now had for the first time in four years the opportunity to appraise the equipment with which passenger service was performed in light of peacetime requirements. As they looked ahead into 1946 and 1947 in terms of motive power for passenger service, there did not appear to be any development of a decidedly radical

nature on the immediate horizon—unless one considered the steam turbine and the application of the gas turbine to locomotive use in that category. The character of motive power in railroad service was always directly related to the problems of operation. During the previous four years there had hardly ever been a time when the operating departments had any more locomotive capacity than was needed for the job at hand. For once, in recent railroad history, the railroads had an opportunity to test out both theories and practices as applied to passenger trains of full car limits operating at high speeds. Not only this, but the passenger traffic volume between January of 1942 and January of 1945 represented the maximum with which operating departments would have to contend for some time to come. So, any idea that passenger motive power would have to be developed for hauling heavier trains faster beyond the train and speed limits of the present was a matter that could be postponed for the moment. But there could be discussion regarding how the refinement of existing designs could produce the coming decade's power.

In any talk on the development of motive power, it was always worthwhile to call attention to the fact that absorption in a study of engineering refinements of existing types could cause one to lose sight of a major factor in railroad operation—that the primary job of a railroad was that of hauling tons of freight and thousands of passenger cars over varying distances and under all kinds of conditions, and, of course, doing it all at a profit. It was of little value in the overall picture if engineering achievement resulted in a locomotive

UNION PACIFIC EMPLOYES BUY "FLYING FORTRESS"

"Spirit Of Union Pacific" Goes To War

Proudly a committee of Union Pacific employes went to Seattle recently to see "our" Flying Fortress off-to-the-wars. Attending the dedication (pictured above, left to right) were: H. O. West, Executive Vice Pres., Boeing Aircraft Co.; Walter Wilson, chairman Union Pacific War Bond Committee; F. W. Madden, representing Brotherhood Railway Clerks; John D. Beard, Brotherhood Maintenance of Way; L. A. Collins, Supt. Oregon Division; D. W. Hood, Brotherhood Railway Trainmen; and A. A. Murphy, Assistant to President of Union Pacific.

To the Employes of the Union Pacific goes the distinction, according to the Treasury Department, of being the first railroad group in the Nation to be honored with a "named" heavy bomber for voluntarily increasing their payroll deductions for War Bonds by more than $379,000 during May and June.

"You have certainly done a grand job on the Union Pacific Bomber Bond Campaign," wrote James L. Houghteling, Director, National Organizations Division, Treasury Dept., War Savings Staff.

of substantially higher thermal efficiency if the cost of building, operating, and maintaining such a power plant was poor in its cost relationship to traffic.

As mentioned, the diesel-electric and the modern steam locomotive had set performance records and cost records that were going to require real engineering development work to improve. The steam turbine, the turbine-electric and the gas-turbine locomotive had not only to compete with the improvements in existing motive power types that were sure to come, but had to be developed in themselves to a point where they could take their place in the every-day job of railroading on a basis of favorable cost relationship. The decreasing first cost of the diesel-electric was rapidly establishing the higher boundaries of initial investment and when the cost of operation on a passenger car-mile basis was considered it became immediately evident that no competing form of motive power that did not have all of the favorable operating and design characteristics that have made the diesel-electric so popular with the operating departments could afford to approach its first cost. The diesel-electric had established many a comparison standard that would remain for some time to come.

For several years and millions of miles of service the passenger diesel had been represented by the 6,000-hp. locomotive, which could be used, as occasion demanded, in 2,000-hp. units. This was the locomotive that had established performance records in all parts of the nation, and, on many roads, had meant the difference between the ability to handle the wartime traffic and failure to handle it. Without these diesels it is difficult to imagine what the result might have been.

A diesel-electric passenger locomotive of improved characteristics had recently been announced by the Electro-Motive Division of General Motors Corporation. The new 6,000-hp. locomotive would have top speeds of 95 mph with 1,500 hp. in a single engine in each of four cab units. The A units would have an overall length of 50 feet 8 inches and the B units 50 feet. The weight of each unit was 230,000 pounds, carried on four axles, giving an axle loading of 57,500 pounds per axle. All of the units would have standard coupler equipment at both ends of the cab making for maximum flexibility of operation. Three other builders of diesel-electric locomotives—Alco-General Electric, Baldwin-Westinghouse, and Fairbanks-Morse—also had designs of locomotives in cab units of 1,500 and 2,000 hp., which would no doubt find their way into road passenger service.

Outstanding among the steam locomotives that had design characteristics which enabled them to perform in a manner that made them powerful factors in the competition between steam and other types of motive power were Pennsylvania's T-1, the New York Central's No. 6000, Class S-1a, and the Norfolk & Western's Class J. But it was Pennsylvania's "experimental" Class T-1 steam locomotive that had the railroad industry by its ears. Designed to average 100 miles an hour with eleven cars weighing 880 tons, it had averaged more than 100 and actually ran more than 130 (on test runs) with sixteen passenger cars weighing nearly 1,200 tons. Its boiler was smaller than that of many engines rated at around 5,000 hp. Yet, it had developed more than 6,500 hp. The first of several steam locomotive projects originating in the resolve of the coal-carrying roads, locomotive builders, and coal industry to combat the growing acceptance of the oil-burning diesel-electric, it had proven so successful that the conservative Pennsylvania (noted for never adopting a new engine design that it had not tested beyond a shadow of a doubt) was spending between $15 and $17 million on fifty engines like it.

The T-1 differed from the comparable conventional steam locomotive in two respects: it had four cylinders instead of two; and it fed steam to the cylinders by means of a new poppet-valve arrangement. The comparable standard passenger locomotive in 1945 was the 4-8-4 type; it had a four-wheel leading truck, four pairs of drivers, and a four-wheel trailing truck. The drivers were driven by a single pair of pistons and connecting rods, which at 100 miles an hour thrashed around seven or more times a second. Even when made of light alloys, the rod assembly weighed as much as three tons, and unless carefully counterbalanced could pound the rail unmercifully. An important advantage of the diesel-electric in high-speed service was that it did not pound the rail.

As early as 1932, the Baldwin Locomotive Works proposed to offset the diesel's advantage by using two pairs of lighter, smaller cylinders and rods instead of one. The idea was not exactly new; for some fifty years railroads had been using two pairs of cylinders on huge freight engines. But they used them with an articulated connection, and only to enable the front set to swivel so the engine could negotiate curves. Baldwin wanted to use two pairs on a rigid frame, primarily to eliminate the pound of the heavy rod assembly, secondarily because it believed two pairs of pistons and valves would handle steam more efficiently than one. So, in 1937, Baldwin, with American Locomotive Co., Lima Locomotive Works, and the Pennsylvania Railroad, designed the great Class S-1 four-cylinder engine ex-

Having served more than 6,000,000 members of the armed forces during its 54 months of operations, the sign of the world-famous Service Men's Canteen in the Union Pacific Railroad station at North Platte, Neb., was taken down April 1, 1946, and the canteen doors locked. Here a workman is shown lowering the sign to Rae Wilson, left, and Mrs. Adam Christ, right, as C. H. Land, bridge and building supervisor for the railroad, steadied the ladder. Miss Wilson opened the canteen Dec. 25, 1941, but the stress of work and responsibility brought on an illness which necessitated her departure for California. Mrs. Christ, wife of a Union Pacific engineer, carried on. Service men from all over the world wrote thousands of thank you letters to the women operating the canteen, which was supported by North Platte groups and 122 Nebraska and Colorado communities and the railroad. UPRR

When the war was over the railroads went back to hauling civilian passengers and cargo. Here is Lehigh Valley Railroad's Engine 2097 all decked out, flags and all, on April 21, 1946. LEHIGH VALLEY

hibited at the World's Fair in 1939 and 1940. And, in 1940, the Pennsylvania ordered two engines somewhat smaller from Baldwin. They were the T-1s, No. 6110 and No. 6111.

In the meantime, the Pennsylvania had been achieving sensational results from an experimental poppet valve developed by the Franklin Railway Supply Company. The main trouble with the conventional piston valve at high speed was that intake and exhaust openings were not adequate and could not be controlled separately. As a result, the exhaust port was often closed before most of the steam was exhausted from the cylinder. The poppet system, using valves somewhat like auto valves, permitted not only independent action of intake and exhaust "events," but more precise control of them. Poppet valves were common in Europe, but experimental applications met with little success in America because they proved troublesome and because few steam engines ran fast enough to justify their higher cost.

Nonetheless, the Franklin people decided to design a set for U.S. service. After a decade of testing and redesigning, they persuaded Pennsylvania to try their system in 1939. With the new valves, a Pennsylvania standard K-4 passenger engine rated at 3,500 hp. developed about 4,200 hp. On one run it hauled a 914-ton train from Warsaw to Liverpool, Indiana, nearly eighty miles at an average of eighty-four miles an hour. Delighted, the Pennsylvania decided to equip the T-1s with Franklin valves. The valves and engines performed so well in nearly three years of experimental operation that the Pennsylvania ordered fifty more—twenty-five from Baldwin and twenty-five from its own Altoona shops. They cost an estimated $300,000 apiece, of which some $30,000 was accounted for by the valve system.

Of course, both Baldwin and Franklin were jubilant. "These locomotives," said Ralph P. Johnson, Baldwin's chief engineer, "will outperform a 5,400-hp. diesel locomotive at all speeds above twenty-six miles per hour, and if given comparable facilities for servicing and maintenance will do the work more cheaply." There was little doubt in anyone's mind that the T-1 would strongly influence the trend of steam-locomotive design in the coming years.

Here Gen. Yoshira Umaze signs the surrender document on behalf of the Japanese Imperial General Headquarters, aboard the battleship USS *Missouri* in Tokyo Bay. Speaking at the microphone is Gen. Douglas MacArthur, to his left Lt. Gen. Richard K. Sutherland. Behind them are senior officers representing the Allies and in the lower right-hand corner are the senior officers of the United States armed forces. With the signing of this document our overburdened railroads could regroup and recover from the shock of the long war years. USASC

A War Job Still To Be Finished

America's railroads handled nearly 44 million members of the armed forces during the 45-month period between Pearl Harbor and the cessation of hostilities with Japan, but, as all railroaders knew, V-J Day did not mean that the carriers were finished with their jobs. Late in 1945 and early in 1946, 6,000,000 service men would be coming home. Ahead was the task of transporting to all parts of the United States the nation's armed forces, which had taken more than three and a half years to build up throughout the world. The demobilization plan called for heavy troop movements continuing through September of 1946, with some of the monthly loads rivaling peak movements during the period of conflict on both fronts.

Furthermore, the troops that would be arriving at the ports would not make one journey home. Depending upon whether they were demobilized or merely given a furlough at home and reassigned for further service in either occupation armies or units destined for the Pacific, these troops would average three to six railroad trips.

The wartime passenger load, handled as it was under conditions of manpower shortages and prohibitions against the acquisition of new equipment, put a severe strain on the carriers with the pinch naturally becoming tighter as time went on. Thus, 1945 became the toughest war year for the rail traveler, bringing additional restrictions on civilian journeys and the so-called "atrocity" stories about accommodations furnished by the railroads for returning service men. Not only this, but 1945 was a year of reiterated "don't travel" appeals, including that issued by President Truman on June 7.

The restrictions, many of them removed since V-J Day, included bans on the transportation of race horses, and on conventions, fairs, trade shows, and group travel. Also, there was the curtailment of facilities for travel to summer camps and school and college athletic camps. In January came the O.D.T. order requiring railroads to discontinue resort trains and establishing a permit system for the operation of any train on which the occupancy of seats and space did not average 35 percent during November 1944. Later, the Navy was required to follow the Army's practice of assigning two men to a lower berth on sleeping cars, while the order prohibiting railroads from selling or allocating space on any passenger train more than five days in advance came along on June 29, although it was eased after V-J Day

to permit reservations 14 days in advance.

Earlier in June the railroads had created a pool of 500 passenger-train cars to be administered by the A.A.R. Car Service Division in an effort to speed up the movement of returning troops. On July 17, the O.D.T. issued its General Order 55, setting up mandatory controls for the assignment of any or all passenger equipment, except sleeping cars, to military use, prescribing procedures similar to those that the railroad had already adopted voluntarily. Meanwhile, on July 7, the O.D.T. had issued its most drastic order of the year—General Order No. 53, which prohibited the operation of sleeping cars on any run of 450 miles or less. This resulted in the withdrawal of 895 sleeping cars from regular civilian runs for the use of military personnel. It brought to 5,000 the number of Pullman sleeping cars thus assigned, leaving only 2,500, or one-third of the entire fleet of 7,500, available to handle all civilian travel. The order was not expected to be greatly eased before the end of the year, when deliveries on the second lot of 1,200 troop sleepers and 400 kitchen cars ordered by the government were scheduled for completion. These two lots of troop sleepers, the first having been delivered sometime in 1944, comprised the only wartime relief received by the railroads in the way of new passenger equipment.

The sleeper ban came at a time when difficulties in connection with the handling of troops were at the most acute stage. It was the period between V-E Day and V-J Day, when all efforts of the military leaders were concentrated on the rapid "redeployment" of the forces in Europe to the Pacific.

It should be noted that during these highly congested months, the streamliners did their jobs, too. Throughout the war, in fact, the modern lightweight trains, maintained a record of handling a vast volume of passenger traffic. In fact, revenues of over $10 per train mile were by no means uncommon. If anything, their popularity increased over the enthusiastic reception that had greeted them from the time the first one was introduced in 1934. That railway executives were by no means unaware of this was indicated by the number of orders for such trains that were placed as soon as passenger cars could be built.

A few changes occurred in streamliner operations during the 1944–45 year. The most important of these was the inauguration of through-streamliner service on the Rock Island, between Minneapolis-St. Paul and Houston. Previous services had been operated over all of this route, but a rearrangement of schedules and equipment permitted the operation of a through-streamliner over the entire 1,370-mile route.

The following list of streamliners remained practically static during the war—because of the prohibition on passenger car building. The list includes only those trains that at their inception consisted entirely of lightweight new equipment. There were, of course,

a large number of rebuilt streamlined trains, operating with so-called standard equipment that had been refurbished. Such trains, too, had accomplished remarkable results in assisting in handling the war-time and post-war passenger traffic.

The aftermath of V-J Day on Market Street in San Francisco. With the ferry building in the far-distant background we see one of San Francisco's Iron Monster street cars, No. 66, heading up Market Street as the sailors and civilians still parade up and down the sidewalks. This view is at California Street & Grant Ave. MOULIN STUDIOS

The Nation's Streamliners

Railway	No. of Trains	Name of Train	Normal Consist	Placed in Service	Operated Between	Daily Mileage Per Train
Alton	1	Abraham Lincoln	12	7-1-35	Chicago-St. Louis	568
	1	Ann Rutledge	12	7-26-37	Chicago-St. Louis	568
A. T. & S. F.	2	Super Chief	12	2-22-38 (a)	Chicago-Los Angeles	636
	6	Chief	13	2-22-38 (a)	Chicago-Los Angeles	743
	2	Kansas Cityan	14	4-17-38	Chicago-Oklahoma	851
	1	Tulsan	6	12-10-39	Kansas City-Tulsa	512
	2	Golden Gate	7	7-1-38	Oakland-Bakersfield	626
	2	San Diegan	13	3-27-38	Los Angeles-San Diego	512
	2	El Capitan	12	2-22-38	Chicago-Los Angeles	636
A. C. L.-F. E. C.	3	Champion	14	12-1-39	New York-Miami (Penna.-R. F. & P.- A. C. L.-F. E. C.)	700
B. & M.-Me. C.	1	Mountaineer (b)	3	4-1-35	Boston-Littleton-Bethlehem	386
C. & E. I.	1	Dixie Flagler	7	12-17-40	Chicago-Miami (C. & E. I.-L. & N.-N. C. & St. L.-A. B. & C.-A. C. L.- F. E. C.)	970
C. & N. W.	2	Twin Cities 400	13	9-24-39 (a)	Chicago-Minneapolis	419
	1	Minnesota 400	5	1-8-42 (a)	Wyeville-Mankato	434
	1	Peninsula 400	13	1-8-42	Chicago-Ishpeming	775
	1	Shoreland 400	7	1-8-42	Chicago-Green Bay	585
	1	Capitol 400	7	1-8-42	Chicago-Madison	651
C. & N. W.-U. P.	1	City of Portland	13	6-6-35	Chicago-Portland	805
	2	City of Los Angeles	14	12-27-37	Chicago-Los Angeles	904
	2	City of Denver	11	6-18-36	Chicago-Denver	1,048
C. & N. W.-U. P.-S. P.	2	City of San Francisco	14	6-14-36	Chicago-Oakland	961
C. B. & Q.	1	Pioneer Zephyr	4	11-11-34	Lincoln-McCook	456
(See also C. R. I. & P.)	1	Mark Twain Zephyr	3	10-28-35	St. Louis-Burlington	442
	2	Denver Zephyr	12	11-8-36	Chicago-Denver	1,037
	2	Twin Zephyr	9	12-18-36	Chicago-Minneapolis	874
	1	Silver Streak Zephyr	4	4-15-40	Lincoln-Kansas City	502
	1	Ak-Sar-Ben Zephyr	8	12-11-40	Lincoln-Chicago	551
	1	Advance Flyer	6	2-2-41	Chicago-Lincoln	551
	2	Texas Zephyr	12	6-2-40	Denver-Dallas	832
C. B. & Q.-C. R. I. & P.	2	Zephyr Rocket	7	1-7-41	St. Louis-Minneapolis	585
	1	Sam Houston Zephyr	5	10-1-36	Houston-Ft. Worth	566
C. M. St. P. & P.	2	Afternoon Hiawatha	12	5-29-35	Chicago-Minneapolis	421
	2	Morning Hiawatha	12	1-21-39	Chicago-Minneapolis	421
	2	Midwest Hiawatha	10	12-11-40	Chicago-Omaha (c)	488
C. R. I. & P.	2	Rocky Mountain Rocket	9	11-12-39	Chicago-Denver (d)	1,084
(See Also C. B. & Q.-	3	Twin Star Rocket	5-7	1-14-45	Minneapolis-Houston (e)	1,368
C. R. I. & P.)	1	Peoria Rocket	4	9-19-37	Chicago-Peoria	644
	1	Des Moines Rocket	6	9-26-37	Chicago-Des Moines	716
	2	Choctaw Rocket	6	11-17-40	Memphis-Amarillo	761
	2	Texas Rocket	4	11-15-38	Kansas City-Dallas (f)	677
F. E. C. (See A. C. L., C. & E. I., I. C. and Penna.)						
G. M. & O.	3	The Rebel	4	7-1-35	New Orleans-St. Louis	751
I. C.	2	Panama Limited	11	5-3-42	Chicago-New Orleans	921
	1	City of Miami	7	12-18-40	Chicago-Miami (I. C.-C. of Ga.-A. C. L.-F. E. C.)	995
	1	Green Diamond	4	5-17-36	Chicago-St. Louis	588
K. C. S.-L. & A.	3	Southern Belle	9	9-1-40	Kansas City-New Orleans	873
M. P.	2	Missouri River Eagle	6	3-10-40	St. Louis-Omaha	478
	2	Colorado Eagle	6	6-21-42	St. Louis-Denver	1,011
	1	Delta Eagle	2	5-11-41	Memphis-Tallulah	518
N. Y. C.	2	Twentieth Century Limited	17	6-15-38 (a)	New York-Chicago	961
	2	Empire State Express	16	12-7-41	New York-Cleveland (g)	872
	1	James Whitcomb Riley	8	4-28-41	Chicago-Cincinnati (h)	605
N. Y. N. H. & H.	1	Comet	3	6-5-35	Greenbush-Whitman	275
Pennsylvania	2	Broadway Limited	15	6-15-38 (a)	Chicago-New York	908
(See also A. C. L., Seaboard and Southern)	1	South Wind	7	12-19-40	Chicago-Miami (Penna.-L. & N.-A. C. L.-F. E. C.)	1,039
Reading	1	Crusader	5	12-13-37	Jersey City-Philadelphia	360
Seaboard	3	Silver Metor	17	2-2-39	New York-Miami (Penna.-R. F. & P.-Seaboard)	1,388
	3	Silver Metor	12	2-2-39	New York-St. Petersburg (Penna.-R. F. & P.-Seaboard)	1,247
Southern	3	Southerner	8	3-31-41	New York-New Orleans (Penna.-Sou.)	924
	3	Tennessean	9	5-17-41	Washington-Memphis (Sou.-N. & W.-Sou.)	619
S. P.	2	Sunbeam	6	9-19-37	Houston-Dallas	264
(See also C. & N. W.)	2	Hustler	13	9-19-37	Houston-Dallas	264
	2	Coast Daylight	20	3-21-37	San Francisco-Los Angeles	470
	2	San Joaquim Daylight	20	7-4-41	Oakland-Los Angeles	479
	2	Lark	20	5-1-41 (a)	San Francisco-Los Angeles	470
U. P. (See C. & N. W.)						

(a) Date lightweight equipment was installed instead of heavy on an existing train.
(b) During winter this train is known as the "Cheshire" and operates between Boston and White River Junction.
(c) Train splits at Manilla, Iowa, one section going to Omaha, another to Sioux Falls.
(d) A streamlined connection is operated between Limon and Colorado Springs.
(e) Operates over B.-R. I. between Dallas and Houston.
(f) Makes a round trip also between El Reno and Oklahoma City.
(g) A connection for this train is operated between Detroit and Buffalo.
(h) Operates over the I. C. between Chicago and Kankakee.

6
....

CONCLUSION:
Plans For The Postwar Traveler

With World War II drawing to a close, what could the traveler expect from railway transportation in the future?

Railroad management and car-builders had been preparing an answer since 1943. Through their advanced planning, attractive accommodations were on the way for the postwar traveler. Color, luxury, speed, and low prices would feature railway passenger service by 1947. The revolutionary suggestions as to color and luxury in passenger cars, as conceived in the engineering departments of the car-builders, were being displayed via such models as the new Astra-Liner planned by the Electro-Motive Division of General Motors. When completed, this bright and revolutionary train would be taken on a tour of the country by its owners in order that its eye-filling appeal would aid in stimulating railway passenger traffic.

Meanwhile, the carriers themselves planned reductions in passenger fares. Schedules were to be shortened as soon as the streamlined equipment and fast passenger locomotives on order were delivered. One of the most interesting proposals was the operation of through-transcontinental streamliners between New York and California. This plan was well beyond the merely speculative stage. Tentative schedules for weekend "sailings" with Friday evening departure and Monday morning arrival had already been made by October of 1945. The proposed trains would be of the luxury type, with all-room accommodations. However, a coach streamliner on such a run was also being discussed.

These plans for passenger service improvements were not based merely on what some railway officers thought the passengers ought to have. On the contrary, there had never been a time when so much study had

been given by the railways as to what the passengers really wanted. For example, as early as 1943, a survey was made by "Railway Age" among the executives of the leading passenger-carrying lines. The five salient points developed in that survey showed a remarkable degree of accurate prophecy. They were:

1) In order to hold as large a share as possible of post-war passenger traffic, the railroads would offer radical new trains of exterior and interior designs;

2) The carriers recognized that most of their present passenger equipment was outmoded and were planning to replace it with modern light-weight equipment as soon as possible. Most companies planned to buy up to the limit of their financial ability;

3) A majority of the railroads favored a reduction in passenger fares after the war;

4) Many railways planned to augment their fleets of coach streamliners materially to add the appeal of frequency of service to the existing advantages of comfort and speed as compared with highway competition;

5) Nearly all of the railroads had made elaborate studies and formulated plans for holding passenger business and the end of the war would not find them unprepared. In some cases, these plans included participation in air transport, if allowed.

When the passengers themselves were asked what they wanted, virtually all agreed that lower fares was the most important priority. In 1945 and 1946, fares for plane travel had been reduced to about 4.5 cents per mile, as compared with basic rail rates of 3.3 cents per mile, first class; tourist class fares of 2.475 cents per mile on certain western railways; and coach fares of 2.2 cents per mile. The 15 percent tax on transportation tickets supplied a slight added differential in favor of rail tickets, but the margin, when Pullman fares were added to first-class, was too close for comfort. Although low fares were important for most travelers, they also expressed a desire for faster rail schedules, greater safety, additional comfort and service on board, better appearance in terms of eye-pleasing pastel colors and indirect-lighting, more lunch-style dining cars, and the introduction of lounge bars, nurseries, motion pictures, barber and beauty shops. Eighty-five percent of all those polled expressed preference for diesel-electric power, stating that diesels afforded smoother and cleaner rides.

But there was little question about it in 1945. In the immediate future, passenger service would be governed to the greatest extent possible by the desires and needs of the passengers. From now on, the customer would be, figuratively, in the driver's seat. Management realized that this was as it should be, and must be, if passengers were not to be literally in the driver's seat — of their private automobiles.

7

....

POSTSCRIPT:
Other Means of Transportation Used in the War Effort

*L*est we forget, electric railroads, local street cars, motor coaches, both local transit and highway, local highway trucks, ferry boats and inland waterways, and airlines all came under the control of the ODT.

One must remember that although the railroads *did* have the burden of carrying people and material during the war years, they were amply assisted by the smaller electric (traction) railroads and other modes of transportation noted above. Without the help of these lesser means of moving people and material the railroads certainly would have been bogged down. So to a lesser degree we must make a little space for them.

Electric traction railroads, such as the Sacramento Northern Railroad operating between Oakland and the Moraga Valley to Sacramento and Chico, carried troops and material from such bases as Camp Beale, Susuin/Fairfield AFB (now Travis AFB), and the large Oakland Army Base along with many lesser military bases.

The government even built a new electric railway line to haul shipyard workers from Emeryville (Oakland), Calif., to the Richmond Shipyards. The Shipyard Railway, as it was called, used old wooden New York City 2nd Ave. elevated cars modified for street operations, which included placing a pantograph on the roof of each motor car. This line operated 24 hours a day during the war years hauling workers back and forth. It was torn up on final victory. One of the two car trains has been preserved and is now located at the California Railway Museum at Rio Vista Jct., Calif.

Another line was the San Francisco Shipyard Railway, which operated a short distance from a site near Candlestick Park to the Hunters Point Shipyards. This train was pulled by a steam engine and the cars consisted of a few New York City elevated railway cars.

San Diego, Calif., exploded overnight. What with a large naval base coupled with a large aircraft industry, it needed wheels to haul military personnel and aircraft workers. To meet these demands ODT supplied San Diego with additional street cars from New York City, Wilkes-Barre and Salt Lake City.

When the Interurban Electric Railway (transbay electric lines of the SP RR) was abandoned in 1941, its cars were not scrapped but stored. When the war came along, the ODT transferred the big RED cars to such places as the Pacific Electric Ry in Southern California, Alabama, Ogden Arsenal, and the Portland Shipyards. All of the steel cars from the Northwestern Pacific RR Marin County suburban lines were transferred to the Pacific Electric Ry.

In what is believed to be the largest fleet of motor buses ever operated for a single government project, during the war years, the Mare Island Naval shipyard operated over 300 motor coaches valued at over 40 million dollars to such long-ranged places as Sacramento, Woodland, San Francisco, Hayward, Oakland, Walnut Creek, Antioch, Calistoga, Healdsburg/Santa Rosa, San Anselmo/Fairfax, San Rafeal/Corte Madera, Sausalito/Mill Valley and many other areas over 32 different lines. Over 25,000 miles operated daily over these 32 lines, hauling shipyard workers 24 hours a day to and from work at the shipyards. More buses were used on this system than were used, at that time,

Sacramento Northern Railroad's #603-604 with #440 pushing on the Lake Temescalgrade out of Oakland, September 1944. Although these short military trains did not compare to the 50- and 100-car trains of the trunk lines, they were important to the war effort because the Sacramento Northern through the Oakland Terminal Railway served the large Oakland Army base's port of embarkation where the ships left for the Pacific war zones.
W.C. WHITAKER

Sacramento Northern RR #440. Even the electric traction railroads hauled military supplies. Here we have a short freight, due to heavy grade out of Oakland, taken on Shafter Ave. in north Oakland ready for the grind over the Oakland hills to Moraga Valley, Walnut Creek and north to Sacramento. Photo taken in 1944. W.C. WHITAKER

. . .

to serve the city of San Francisco. Many of these buses were driven by women.

To give an example of the different sizes of these military-operated bus lines, take Crane Naval Ammunition Depot, located to the west of Bloomington, Indiana, the home of Indiana University. Crane NAD, at that time, was the largest Naval Ammunition Depot in the world covering approximately 125 square miles. At one point it was ten miles across the base, at least over the roads that the buses operated on. This base had a medium-sized motor bus operation within the base, as well as a line that ran into Bloomington. In 1944 they had at least six diesel/electric motor coaches, originally ordered and built for the 5th Ave. Motor Coach Line of New York City. When the war came, the ODT allotted these diesels to Crane NAD to supplement the fleet of smaller school-type buses they had.

Crane also operated a number of tractor-type trucks, which hauled trailers modified to carry people instead of material. Although these trailers were outlawed in most states, they were allowed to run over the public highways when and where needed because of the war.

These are only two of the hundreds, or I should say thousands, of bus operations set up during the war years. It was operations like these, throughout the nation, that released rail equipment for the railroads to use on their more important task—getting the troops and materials to the war fronts.

In addition, Crane NAD had a large railroad complex, over 100 miles of track serving the various storage areas, plus rail connection with the CMStP&P at Burns City. Diesel locomotives were used on this vast operation along with a small number of demotorized 2nd Ave. Elevated Railroad passenger cars from New York

SN #604-603 with #440 westbound downgrade through Pinehurst Canyon in the Oakland Hills. She has just come out of the tunnel from Redwood Canyon and is heading for the Oakland Army Base. Due to steep grades freight trains through this area were quite small. Sept. 1944. W.C. WHITAKER

Pennsylvania Railroad's Philadelphia suburban lines were handled by heavy electric trains as shown in this pre-war photo of a six-car train taken in September 1938. PRR

· · ·

City. These cars were used to haul the workers to and from work throughout the base. The CMStP&P ran a special workers train, made up of old heavyweight wooden passenger coaches, down from Terre Haute. This train ran right onto the base.

Again, railroad operations within the many military bases throughout the country operated during the war years. Civilians never knew of many of these operations, and, indeed, today I'll wager that many of them have been long forgotten and their existence lost to history.

With regard to trucks and trucking, not many trucks were built during the war years for civilian use, thus many old 1920–1930 era trucks were operated during the war years. Even trucks manufactured by what once was the largest truck manufacturer in the country, Fageol Motors of Oakland, Calif., went out of business in the early 1930s, ran over the country's highway in 1942–45. Peterbilt Motors, successor of Fageol Motors, built civilian trucks only during the war years, thus there was a small percentage of new trucks on the highways, but not many. Peterbilt did not build anything for the military during the war years.

Ferry boats, especially those in San Francisco Bay,

Puget Sound, and the Port of New York, did come under control of the ODT. These mostly old-time wooden vessels did their share in moving people across bodies of water, mostly in connection with a rail operation. Thus, they were important to the railroads. Even San Francisco Bay with its two giant bridges needed the Southern Pacific RR ferry boats with their train connections. Indeed, the military itself garnered together a fleet of river and ferry boats in San Francisco Bay to help transport troops from Camp Stoneman at Pittsburgh, Calif., to the ships in the bay. They used the Delta King and the Delta Queen; they also brought up one of the Catalina Island ferry boats to operate on San Francisco Bay, plus a few of the old Key System ferry boats, along with a string of Sacramento and San Joaquin river boats and San Francisco Bay ferry boats. This fleet moved military personnel and supplies, and was used as mobile living quarters for war workers and military personnel.

The Civilian Airlines also came under control of the ODT, although small in comparison with the railroads, they did carry large numbers of military personnel who had to be at a destination in a hurry. The DC-3 was the backbone of air transportation in the war years.

Greyhound Motor Coach #279 was just one of the thousands of motor coaches that came under government control with the bombing of Pearl Harbor. This Pacific Greyhound coach was snapped on the San Francisco Embarcadero, just south of the world-famous Ferry Building, whose clock indicates this shot was taken at 11:49 a.m. RNE

One of the first buses built under the General Motors Corp. "GMC" name Sequoia Stages #52 was allotted by the ODT to the Navy. She was assigned to Camp Parks, Pleasanton, Calif., where she ran between Camp Parks and the Naval Air Facility (Anti-submarine Blimp Base) at Livermore, Calif. This operation was separate from the Mare Island Naval Shipyard operation, one of the many small transit operations on military bases throughout the country. This shot was taken at Sequoia Stages Yards on lower University Ave., Berkeley, Calif., circa 1947. EASTSHORE LINES

ODT bus 9150, here as Key System (Oakland, Calif.) #920, shows the lack of chrome and other finery on these wartime-built motor coaches. Although painted in the bright orange & white of the Key System, she was the same bus operated by the military in its drab navy blue or army olive color. RNE

Once the war started the ODT took over all transportation in the country. This Lake Shore Coach Co. bus was an ODT-designed no-frills motor coach.
GMC, WILLIAM BILLINGS COLLECTION

This ODT-designed bus sits outside the General Motors Plant waiting for assignment by the ODT. These transit-type buses lacked the chrome and finery of a peacetime-built vehicle, but they certainly served the war effort. GMC, WILLIAM BILLINGS COLLECTION

Six-unit shipyard railway train on section of old interurban electric railway right-of-way in Berkeley, Calif. These 2nd Ave. obsolete elevated cars from New York City ran for almost four years, 24 hours a day, every day of the year. JOE CHAPMAN

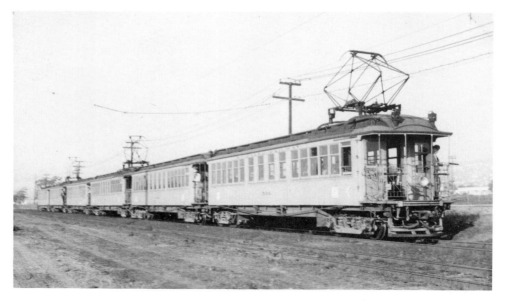

New York City trolley on the streets of San Diego. Very early in the war it was apparent that the city of San Diego, Calif., needed additional street cars to serve the military personnel. New York City had some spare cars that the ODT transferred to San Diego, along with some from Salt Lake City and Wilkes-Barre. Here we have 3rd Ave. Ry of NYC #473 in her revenue service on the streets of San Diego in 1942. RNE

Saved from the scrap pile, these five high-speed interurban cars from the Sacramento Northern Railway were saved and used as a train unit on the transbay lines of the key system. Snapped on Shattuck Ave. in Berkeley. RNE

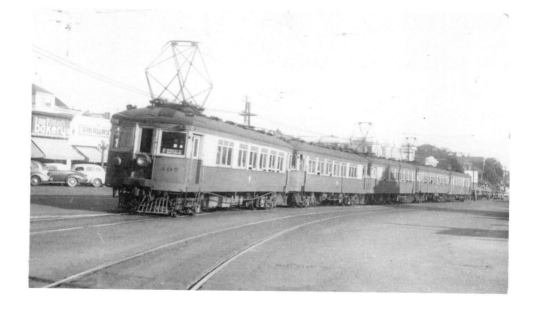

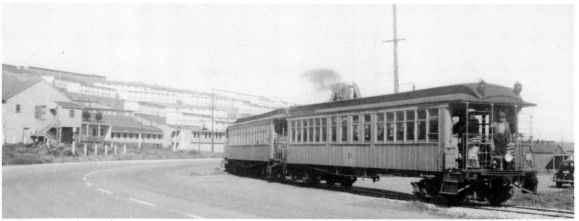

San Francisco shipyard railway train taking curve near Hunters Point. This short rail operation, which ran during the war years, carried workers to their jobs at Hunters Point in the Candlestick Cover district of San Francisco. This was a steam operation with a light tank engine pulling old New York City "El" non-motorized trailers. Cars were painted navy gray. WARREN K. MILLER PHOTO

Key System 498, head-end of the five-car unit train operated by the Key System during the war years on the "F" Albany-Berkeley-Emeryville and over the SF-Oakland Bay Bridge line to San Francisco. These former Sacramento Northern cars were saved from the scrap heap and did their part toward the war effort. Color of cars was the Key System Orange & White. WARREN K. MILLER PHOTO

Key System trolley #911 advertises the need for blood during the war years. Snapped in 1944 in Emeryville, Calif. RNE

. . .

Even the railroads operated trucks. Pacific Motor Transport #809, owned and operated by the SP RR at Merced, Calif., date unknown. The SP operated these trucks up and down the West Coast, especially in areas where they abandoned rail service. RNE

Even some Fageols were on the highways during World War II. This is one of the last models built by Fageol in Oakland, Calif., before the plant was taken over by Peterbilt. RNE

A General Motors truck with a shipment of Golden Glow Ale at Oakland, Calif. RNE

Paddle wheeler "Crockett" with her two stacks and paddle wheel sits in the water at Stockton, Calif., just prior to the war. She, like all of the other river boats, was pressed intogovernment service once the war was started. This photograph, taken by George Henderson, shows her before being painted the wartime navy gray. RNE

USS YHB-25 was the former SP ferry boat "Alameda" sitting at the service dock of the Oakland Mole. Painted in the drab navy gray the Alameda did her share in moving troops around the bay in the war years. This view was taken in 1943 at the height of her war service.

Southern Pacific Railroad's "Sacramento" paddling her way across the bay to the Oakland Mole was one of the prime movers, along with the other SP ferry boats, of people across the bay during the war years. This Joe Chapman photo shows the paddle wheel movement, along with part of the SF-Oakland Bay Bridge in the background. These ferry boats met all of the SP & WP passenger trains at the Oakland Mole to expedite the passengers onto "Bagdad by the bay," San Francisco, Calif. RNE

. . .

This view taken in the late 1930s on Treasure Island in San Francisco Bay shows a Pan American Clipper seaplane on display before her run to Hawaii and points west. Along with the domestic DC3s, the clippers were the backbone of civilian air transport just prior and during the war years. Part of the SF-Oakland Bay bridge can be seen in this shot. RNE

San Joaquin River paddle wheeler sits in the old SP-Golden Gate Auto Ferry slip at the foot of Hyde Street (the current site of the San Francisco Maritime Museum) waiting to be sold by the government after the war. RNE

8
....

Photographs, Charts, Wartime Ads

N&W engine 500 with passenger
train "Pocohontas" leaving Norfolk,
Va. NW

The elaborate Union Station Terminal at Cincinnati, Ohio, was a busy place during the war. The building is now a museum. C&O HISTORICAL SOCIETY

C&O passengers in line at the ticket window inside the C&O-SAL Main Street Station in Richmond, Virginia, 1943. C&O HISTORICAL SOCIETY

CALIFORNIA STATE RAILROAD MUSEUM, SACRAMENTO, CALIFORNIA

Staging yards, like this scene, were located throughout the country. Here are railroad tank cars stored for shipment overseas. With 9906 gallons capacity each, they were ready to be shipped anywhere in the world when needed. In the background are stored steam locomotives ready for shipment where needed. ERIE RR

Loading rack at a mid-continent refinery. LC-USW3-10047-D

Women were employed to work on many of America's railroads. UTAH STATE HISTORICAL SOCIETY

Here WP 203, 2-6-6-2, seems to be in a little trouble as she is being re-railed with the help of two steam derricks at about 3 p.m., Oct. 30, 1943. Except for the trailing truck wheels, the entire engine is suspended between two wrecking cranes. The rear end of the engine was steadied over the rails by the motionless crane at the left, while the crane to the right attempts to swing laterally in an effort to align the front end engine truck wheels over the rails. The lateral movement of the boom swings the truck with ease, but the front of the boiler several times threatened to slide off sideways during this maneuver. WP RR

Locomotives, tank cars, and other necessary units are stored on every available piece of rail in the British Isles. The backup force of railroad equipment would be needed once the invasion took place to keep the armed forces supplied as they moved across France. The two main tracks were kept open for the movement of material and people, but the passing tracks, spurs, branch lines, etc., were all used to store the large number of rail material shipped from the states. These large type 280s, kept under constant guard, were ready for trans-shipment to the continent. This photo was snapped March 15, 1944. USA

An Army officer looks down at a rail yard in the 756th Railway Shop Branch, EBBW Junction Supply Depot, Newport, Wales, where the locomotives are being checked before being put into storage awaiting the invasion of the Europe a few months later. March 15, 1944. USA

. . .

IMPROVEMENT IN FREIGHT TRANSPORTATION

AVERAGE	WORLD WAR I (1918)	WORLD WAR II (1942)	CHANGE
FREIGHT CAR CAPACITY	41.6 TONS	50.5 TONS	+21%
TONS CARRIED PER FREIGHT TRAIN	565 TONS	1,031 TONS	+82%
SPEED OF FREIGHT TRAIN	11.5 MILES P.H.	15.9 MILES P.H.	+38%

GRAPHICS BY PICK-S

PROGRESS IN TROOP TRANSPORTATION

THE AMERICAN RAILROADS CARRIED

IN WORLD WAR I	IN WORLD WAR II
5,000,000 SOLDIERS	11,000,000 SOLDIERS
IN	IN
20 MONTHS	13 MONTHS

PASSENGER TRANSPORTATION

AVERAGE	WORLD WAR I (1918)	WORLD WAR II (1942)	CHANGE
NUMBER OF PASSENGER CARS	53,941	45,000 EST.	-17%
PASSENGERS CARRIED PER YEAR	1,084,997,896	650,000,000 EST.	-40%
TRIP PER PASSENGER	39.33 MILES	75.0 MILES	+91%

MILES OF ROAD IN THE UNITED STATES
ALL LINE-HAUL RAILROADS BY STATES (As of Dec. 31, 1945)

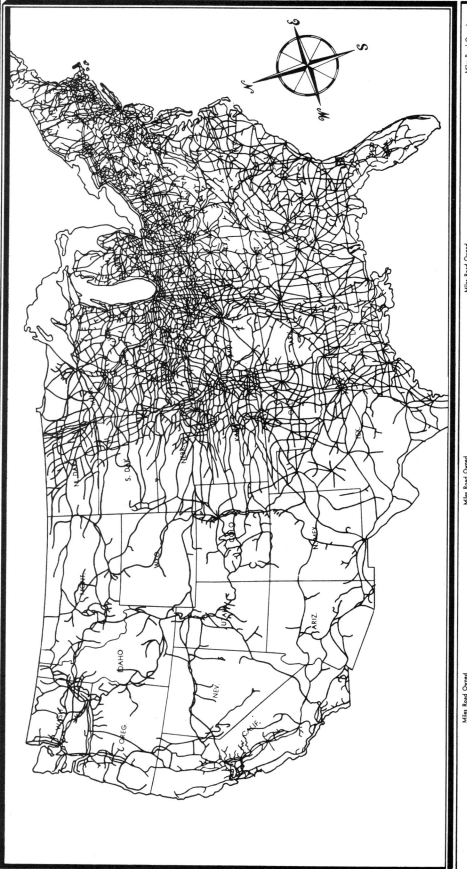

State	Miles Road Owned December 31, 1945
ALABAMA	4,848
ARIZONA	2,209
ARKANSAS	4,354
CALIFORNIA	7,383
COLORADO	4,425
CONNECTICUT	875
DELAWARE	295
FLORIDA	4,913
GEORGIA	6,190
IDAHO	2,720
ILLINOIS	11,760
INDIANA	6,711

State	Miles Road Owned December 31, 1945
IOWA	8,781
KANSAS	8,445
KENTUCKY	3,578
LOUISIANA	4,151
MAINE	1,827
MARYLAND	1,324
MASSACHUSETTS	1,723
MICHIGAN	6,954
MINNESOTA	8,343
MISSISSIPPI	3,805
MISSOURI	6,876
MONTANA	5,057

State	Miles Road Owned December 31, 1945
NEBRASKA	5,821
NEVADA	1,827
NEW HAMPSHIRE	951
NEW JERSEY	2,044
NEW MEXICO	2,526
NEW YORK	7,629
NORTH CAROLINA	4,534
NORTH DAKOTA	5,266
OHIO	8,417
OKLAHOMA	5,991
OREGON	3,310
PENNSYLVANIA	9,934

State	Miles Road Owned December 31, 1945
RHODE ISLAND	190
SOUTH CAROLINA	3,329
SOUTH DAKOTA	3,981
TENNESSEE	3,494
TEXAS	15,685
UTAH	1,880
VERMONT	903
VIRGINIA	4,110
WASHINGTON	5,227
WEST VIRGINIA	3,747
WISCONSIN	6,395
WYOMING	1,924
DISTRICT OF COLUMBIA	34
TOTAL	226,696

NO NAPPING IN NAPLES

Five days after the American Fifth Army had driven the Germans out of Naples, a ranking Army officer and his experts surveyed a scene of super desolation, then ordered enlisted American railroaders of the Army Transportation Corps to "build two and a half miles of double track between the Naples yards and the docks, and have the trains running in five days!"

American tracklayers and fellow maintenance men had arrived with a few locomotives, rails, and knocked-down box cars—brought in on troop transports and cargo vessels. But they hadn't brought nearly enough.

The wreckage of Naples was a thousand times worse than they had imagined— ruined roadbed, twisted rails, and a hundred cars up-ended on a scrap-heap locomotive. A hundred miles of rails had been torn up, 4000 box cars were matchwood; 600 tank cars, in pieces, blocked what had been railroad yards and main lines.

With German thoroughness the identical sides of twenty locomotives had been blown out, ruining all possibility of repair. Hundreds of rails were wrapped around telegraph poles, even when held together with switch plates. Frogs and switchpoints had been destroyed with diabolical skill.

The Army Transportation Corps went cautiously to work bulldozing dirt and cinders into fifteen-foot craters, while doughboys watched the once derided "pick-and-shovel gang" go over every foot of the landscape with minesweepers. Each sweeper, looking like a plate fastened to the end of a broom stick, was swung back and forth over ground pregnant with death. When the wired plate hummed, a Corps man "deloused" that mine.

Sometimes it was just a can-like, three-pronged "Bouncing Betty" which, when stepped on, leaped three feet into the air and showered soldiers with 300 steel bullets. Sometimes it was a Teller Mine, laid just under ground, enough explosive to blow a jeep to bits.

The transplanted American railroaders had to go easy but fast in the wake of these sweepers!

When they couldn't straighten out German-wrecked rails, the Corps crews used their own American rails, joint bars, tie plates, spikes, switchpoints, and frogs. Unable to repair wrecked locomotives, they used their own. And when German machine guns or the Luftwaffe strafed them, they dived into fox holes or behind wreckage, until the worst of the shooting was over.

But they did their job, ahead of schedule, and combat divisions rolled from bayside into Naples and on toward Rome.

—The Trackwalker*

★ ★ ★

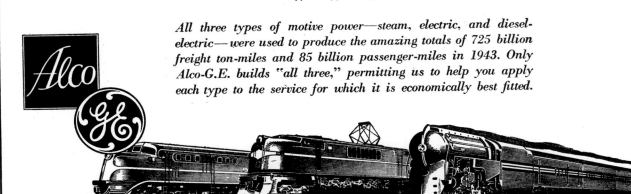

All three types of motive power—steam, electric, and diesel-electric—were used to produce the amazing totals of 725 billion freight ton-miles and 85 billion passenger-miles in 1943. Only Alco-G.E. builds "all three," permitting us to help you apply each type to the service for which it is economically best fitted.

AMERICAN LOCOMOTIVE ● GENERAL ELECTRIC

Copr., 1944, American Locomotive Company and General Electric Company   **Reg. U.S. Pat. Off.*   118-81-9500

Suggestions FOR CIVILIAN TRAVELERS

The Progressive
UNION PACIFIC RAILROAD
ROAD OF THE STREAMLINERS AND CHALLENGERS

Alhambra, Calif.....................121 W. Main St.
Atlanta, Ga........................1232 Healey Building

Bend, Ore..........................112 Oregon Ave.
Boise, Ida...City Ticket Office, Idaho Bldg., 212 No. 8th St.
Boston, Mass...208 Old South Bldg., 294 Washington St.
Bremerton, Wash...Consolidated Ticket Office, 228 First St.
Butte, Mont.....609 Metals Bank Bldg., 8 West Park St.

Chicago, Ill........City Ticket Office, One So. LaSalle St.
Cincinnati, O...303 Dixie Term. Bldg., 4th and Walnut Sts.
Cleveland, Ohio...1916 Terminal Tower, 50 Public Square

Dallas, Texas...1029 Kirby Bldg., Main and Akard Sts.
Denver, Colo......City Ticket Office, 535 Seventeenth St.
Des Moines, Iowa...407 Equitable Bldg., 6th & Locust Sts.
Detroit, Mich....
　　　508 Transportation Bldg., 131 Lafayette Blvd., West.

East Los Angeles, Calif........5454 Ferguson Drive.
Eugene, Ore.........................362 19th Ave. E.

Fresno, Calif.....................207 Rowell Building

Glendale, Calif...City Ticket Office, 206 North Brand Blvd.

Hollywood, Calif...City Ticket Office, 6702 Hollywood Blvd.
Huntington Park, Calif...
　　.............City Ticket Office, 6815 Pacific Blvd.

Kansas City, Mo., City Ticket Office, 208 East 11th Street

Lewiston, Idaho.................Room 7, Union Depot
Lincoln, Nebr.......City Ticket Office, 130 So. 13th St.
Long Beach, Calif...City Ticket Office, 144 Pine Avenue
Los Angeles, Calif..
　　City Ticket Office, Union Pacific Bldg., 434 W. 6th St.

Milwaukee, Wis...814 Warner Bldg., 212 W. Wisconsin Ave.
Minneapolis, Minn.....890 Northwestern Bank Building

New Orleans, La........504 Canal Bldg., 210 Baronne St.
New York, N. Y...
　　.......626 Fifth Ave., Suite 350, Rockefeller Center

Oakland, Calif......215 Central Bank Bldg., 436 14th St.
Ogden, Utah...City Ticket Office, Ben Lomond Hotel Bldg.
Omaha, Nebr.......City Ticket Office, 1614 Farnam St.
　　.............City Ticket Office, Cor. 15th & Dodge Sts.

Pasadena, Calif...Union Pacific Station, 205 W. Colorado St.
Philadelphia, Pa...
　　904 Girard Trust Bldg., Broad St. and So. Penn Square
Pittsburgh, Pa...
　　216 Oliver Bldg., Smithfield Street and Sixth Avenue
Portland, Ore...City Ticket Office, 701 S. W. Washington St.

Reno, Nev...200 Lyon Bldg., Second and Center Streets

St. Joseph, Mo......City Ticket Office, 517 Francis Street
St. Louis, Mo...1223 Ambassador Bldg., 411 No. 7th St.
Sacramento, Calif...217 Forum Bldg., 1107 Ninth Street
Salt Lake City, Utah...City Ticket Office, Hotel Utah Bldg.
San Diego, Calif.....City Ticket Office, 320 Broadway
San Francisco, Calif...
　　.....City Ticket Office, at Geary and Powell Streets
San Jose, Calif.................206 1st Natl. Bank Building
San Pedro, Calif...City Ticket Office, 805 So. Pacific Avenue
Santa Ana, Calif...City Ticket Office, 305 North Main St.
Santa Monica, Calif...
　　.....City Ticket Office, 307 Santa Monica Boulevard
Seattle, Wash.........City Ticket Office, 1300 4th Ave.
Sioux City, Iowa...405 Commerce Bldg., 520 Nebraska St.
Spokane, Wash...City Ticket Office, 727 Sprague Ave.

Tacoma, Was...City Ticket Office, 114 South Ninth St.
Toronto, Ont...201-2 Canadian Pacific Bldg., 69 Yonge St.
Tulsa, Okla...823 Kennedy Bldg., 321 South Boston St.

Walla Walla, Wash...1st Nat'l Bank Bldg., 2nd & Alder Sts.
Washington, D. C...........1019 National Press Building
Winston-Salem, N. C.............632 Reynolds Building

Yakima, Wash...Union Pacific Bldg., 104 W. Yakima Ave.

IT'S the responsibility and patriotic duty of all railroads to handle the transportation of troops and war supplies. At the same time, we are doing our best to provide adequate service for civilian travelers. You can help us to give that service . . . help Uncle Sam, your neighbors and yourself . . . by following these suggestions:

1 When travel is heavy, as it generally is today, patrons frequently may find it difficult to get the accommodations they prefer. Perhaps *no* space will be available. You can help to remedy this condition by cancelling reservations promptly when your travel plans are changed. If all patrons will adopt this suggestion, everyone will benefit.

2 When making reservations, before departure or while en route, ask about new Pullman reservations rule now in effect on all railroads. These regulations were established for the common good.

3 When packing for a trip, put just the articles needed on the train in one bag. Additional luggage, up to 150 pounds, can be checked through in the baggage car—without charge. You'll have more space and less inconvenience. It is advisable that the checking-through of baggage be arranged the day before your departure.

4 When patronizing the Dining Car, please remember that our facilities (Dining Car and Kitchen space) were set up for peace-time and not heavy war-time traffic. Your consideration in relinquishing your seat promptly when you have finished dining will be appreciated by fellow-travelers

5 When planning a trip, make arrangements in advance rather than waiting until arrival at the depot. When trains are departing, the depot ticket-sellers are usually busy and pressed for time. In almost all major cities there are conveniently located ticket offices where our travel experts have more time to help you arrange itineraries, make reservations, etc. Also try to plan departures in mid-week and avoid heavy week-end traffic.

Please consider these suggestions as a friendly effort on our part to make your train trips as pleasant as possible under existing war-time conditions. We have a very vital job to perform and your understanding and cooperation will help us immensely to "keep 'em rolling" for Victory.

C. J. COLLINS
Gen'l Passenger Traffic Manager
Union Pacific Railroad
Omaha, Nebraska

. . .

Railroads make every effort to keep the trains on time. They would like to furnish seats for all and to provide a full choice of Pullman accommodations. To do so under present conditions is sometimes impossible.

Passengers, almost without exception, have recognized the extreme burden which the war has laid upon the railroads, and have met the inconveniences of war-time travel with tolerance and good nature which are sincerely appreciated by the railroads . . . and gratefully acknowledged.

When your trip is necessary—

AVOID WEEK-ENDS
Do your traveling in the middle of the week whenever possible.

TRAVEL LIGHT
Limit your hand baggage to actual requirements. Other baggage can be checked.

PLANS CHANGED?
Cancel your reservation promptly if your trip is deferred or called off.

Association of AMERICAN RAILROADS

THINK *before you travel* ★

EVERY MONTH—two million members of our armed forces board American railroad trains under military orders to ride away on sombre, terrible, necessary business—the business of America's salvation—the business of war.

To move these two million men each month in special cars and trains takes more than one-half of all the sleeping cars and one-third of all the coaches in the United States.

With what equipment is left the railroads must move individual servicemen or smaller groups traveling under orders — soldiers, sailors, marines and coast guards on furlough — families visiting servicemen in camps — businessmen and other workers on war business—those who can no longer use their automobiles—and every other sort of traveler by rail.

In all, the railroads today carry *nearly four times the passenger traffic of 1939.*

That's the score today, and Americans who know it understand why travelers sometimes have to wait at ticket windows, why they cannot always get accommodations when they want them, why coaches are crowded, and trains are sometimes late.

★ ★ ★

Whether you travel this summer — and where — and when, are questions which you alone can answer—but answer them with your eyes fixed on the fighting fronts and with the needs of the armed forces in your mind.

. . .

front seat; at other times he will want to play with his toys or take a nap in the back seat. It will help to keep him amused if you can think up stories to tell him about the things he sees along the way—the children, the cattle, the trains, and the factories. Songs you know by heart will be used many times over, too.

A job this traveling with babies in wartime! Certainly not something to attempt lightly. But if you must travel with your baby, you'll be doing a real war service if you make it as painless as you can to the transportation system, your baby, and yourself.

The Bureau gratefully acknowledges the work of Mr. Gluyas Williams, who illustrated this booklet as a contribution to the war effort.

UNITED STATES DEPARTMENT OF LABOR

FRANCES PERKINS, *Secretary*

CHILDREN'S BUREAU

KATHARINE F. LENROOT, *Chief*

Children in Wartime No. 6   Bureau Publication 307

For sale by the Superintendent of Documents, U. S. Government Printing Office
Washington 25, D. C. . Price 5 cents

If your *baby* must travel in wartime

TO OUR PATRONS:

As a result of point value rationing, our allotment of food has been drastically reduced and it has been necessary to limit dining car service to two meals a day. Breakfast service will be extended until 12:00 noon and dinner service will begin at 4:30 P. M. There will be no luncheon service.

This situation developing as a war necessity we are sure will be understood and appreciated by our patrons.

UNION PACIFIC RAILROAD

Geared to this War of MOVEMENT

On the move . . . that's the order for the U. S. A. . . . on our way to Victory Day! Materials must move, and keep moving . . . military, industrial and civilian needs are mounting daily. The burden of movement is on the nation's railroads.

Frisco Faster Freight is maintaining dependable freight schedules transporting the ever-increasing load with commendable efficiency. Always Frisco Faster Freight has recognized the need of speed and careful handling . . . today, there's a decided step-up in tempo to keep 'em moving faster!

THE FAMOUS FLEET OF FRISCO FLASHES

THE DIXIE FLASH
Early morning delivery from Memphis to Birmingham . . . direct connections at Memphis from Texas, Arkansas, Oklahoma and West . . . to the Carolinas, Florida, Georgia and Alabama.

THE TEXAS FLASH
St. Louis and Kansas City to Dallas and Ft. Worth.

OKLAHOMA FLASH
St. Louis to Tulsa and Oklahoma City.

The only Railroad Serving both Southeast and Southwest with its own rails

THE CUNEO PRESS, INC., CHICAGO, ILL.

24

Printed in U. S. A.

Stars and Bars

On the left sleeve of the uniform worn by passenger conductors, brakemen and flagmen are the insignia indicating length of service; a star for twenty-five years, a bar for each five years.

The proud possessors of "stars and bars" help to form the solid foundation of a railroad's personnel. Because of their intimate knowledge of operating rules, equipment and facilities... the many situations and problems they have met and solved . . . they are of tremendous assistance to younger men.

Among the 65,000 Union Pacific employes there are approximately 7,000 "old timers"— representing all departments — with twenty or more years of service. These experienced employes have, in a large measure, been responsible for the enviable record maintained by Union Pacific in the face of wartime conditions.

The transportation of many thousand trainloads of troops and materials over the Strategic Middle Route, uniting the East with the West Coast, calls for the wisdom and cool judgment of maturity coupled with the ambition and tireless energy of younger employes.

Union Pacific is proud of *all* its employes, regardless of length of service, for the job they are doing to help speed the hour of victory.

Listen to "YOUR AMERICA" radio program on Mutual nationwide network every Sunday afternoon. Consult your local newspaper for the time and station.

THE PROGRESSIVE
UNION PACIFIC
RAILROAD

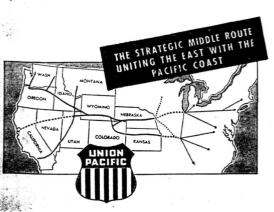

THE STRATEGIC MIDDLE ROUTE UNITING THE EAST WITH THE PACIFIC COAST

Wartime Guide to Grand Central Terminal

STEP FROM the busy heart of New York into the cathedral-like beauty of Grand Central Terminal...and watch the smooth flow of wartime America on the move.

Beneath this high, blue-vaulted ceiling now pass some 54,000,000 travelers a year. Boys on their way to war...watched to the train gates by bravely smiling parents. Workers journeying to strange new war jobs in faraway cities. Business leaders speeding to win new war production battles.

Together they form part of the greatest military and civilian traffic that America's railroads have ever carried. A tremendous task, vital to Victory, and rich in promise for the future.

Out of this experience will be born the finer rail transport of tomorrow ... when Grand Central Terminal will echo to the footsteps and laughter of a free, victorious people bound on swift errands of peace.

❶ 14,800 QUESTIONS AN HOUR

During a busy wartime hour, Terminal information men answer 14,800 questions. To save holding up ticket lines, get information *in advance* at this booth or by telephone.

❷ GRAND CENTRAL SERVICE FLAG

This flag honors 21,314 New York Central employees. Thousands of other Central workers have sons and daughters in uniform...an added drive behind this railroad's war effort.

❸ TICKET OFFICE 90% BUSIER

New York Central has added extra windows and personnel to meet the war rush. Even so, war-wise travelers prefer to buy tickets during quieter mid-morning and early evening hours.

❹ SERVICE MEN'S LOUNGE

Busiest on weekends when thousands travel on furlough. To give them room on weekend trains, plan trips you *must* make for *mid-week*.

❺ 54,000,000 PASSENGERS A YEAR

A record number of essential wartime passengers now flows through Grand Central train gates. Fighters, workers, Government and industrial leaders ... bound on vital errands along the "Warpath of the United Nations."

❻ BAGGAGE CHECKING COUNTER

Some 150,000 pieces of baggage a month are now checked through Grand Central. People have learned to travel light, checking larger luggage, carrying only *one small grip* on crowded trains.

❼ TROOPS ON THE MOVE

Today, half the nation's Pullmans and 30% of its coaches are needed to move 2,000,000 troops per month. One more reason railroads can't always provide the accommodations you want.

❽ THE COMMUTER'S STATION

Grand Central Terminal's Lower Level is principally the commuter's station. Now in war time it is busier than ever because thousands of former automobile travelers must be carried by train.

❾ MAIN WAITING ROOM

Here someone (perhaps a soldier on furlough) may have to wait over for a later train if *you* fail to cancel an unwanted reservation. These days, cancel reservations the *minute* your plans change.

FREE GUIDE TO GRAND CENTRAL

Packed with stories, pictures and a large fascinating detailed cutaway view that takes you behind the scenes of this great Terminal in war time. Write Passenger Dept., Room 1261 J, 466 Lexington Ave., New York, N. Y.

New York Central

ONE OF AMERICA'S RAILROADS — ALL UNITED FOR VICTORY

NEW YORK CENTRAL SYSTEM

BUY MORE WAR BONDS AND STAMPS

"Have a Heart, Pal!"

"SURE, YOU NEED A VACATION. You deserve one, too!

"But have a heart, will you? Go easy on the traveling and leave *some* room on trains for us.

"We'd appreciate that—'cause we'd *like* to get home as fast as we can to make the most of our furloughs.

"And we *have* to be back in camp on time—ready to shove off and do that job you're counting on us to do!"

TO TRAINS →

PULLMAN

● For more than 80 years, the greatest name in passenger transportation—now carrying out mass troop movements with *half* its fleet of sleeping cars and carrying more passengers in the *other* half than the *whole fleet* carried in peacetime!

BUY an EXTRA WAR BOND with what your trip would cost!

Loaded for War

Take a good look at the picture below. It shows a Santa Fe train loaded for war.

That war train is ready to roll. It is *going through.*

In railroad language, it has the right-of-way over everything else on the line. .

So it must be with *all* American transportation until this war job is done.

Victory Rides on Wheels

For this is essentially a war of rolling wheels . . .

Millions of men and millions of tons of vital foods, raw materials, and finished products must be moved swiftly and surely, where and when they are needed.

Stop the wheels that move them, and we stop all that floats and flies as well.

That is why, on the Santa Fe, movements essential to the war effort are topping the greatest transportation job in all our history. They *must* come first, beyond argument or selfish interest.

★ During 1942, *with 26% fewer locomotives,* Santa Fe moved 122% *more freight ton-miles,* and 79% *more* military and civilian passenger-miles than in 1918, during the First World War. The War Department, the ODT, and civilian shippers and travelers everywhere are cooperating 100% with the railroads of America in making records like this possible.

SERVING THE SOUTHWEST FOR 75 YEARS

Santa Fe

"Out of Your Range, Nazi"

When Hitler's packs of undersea wolves struck at domestic shipping along our shores, he forgot about the American railroads — and thereby started driving more spikes into his coffin.

When Axis submarines struck, the Nation's railroads were called upon to move the major part of the oil supply for the East from Southwestern producing centers; to bring Pacific Coast lumber and the bulk of Pacific Coast canned goods to the East; to more than double the all-rail movement of bituminous coal from Southern Appalachian fields into New England; and to transport many other unexpected and unaccustomed loads. Result: today, the greater part of coastwise and intercoastal traffic is being moved safely and efficiently by the all-rail route, and hundreds of vitally needed tankers and other ships have been diverted direct to war purposes.

The Norfolk and Western Railway is carrying its full share of that essential traffic which formerly moved by water. Here's just one example: during the first eight months of 1942, this railroad moved over its Shenandoah Valley line — Roanoke, Va., to Hagerstown, Md. — approximately 2,000,000 tons of bituminous coal consigned to Northern and New England States — 2,000,000 tons of coal diverted from the Port of Norfolk and the water route to N. & W. rails — rails that are out of your range — Nazi.

FOR VICTORY BUY UNITED STATES WAR BONDS AND STAMPS

Norfolk and Western Railway

PRECISION TRANSPORTATION

COPR. 1942 N. & W. RY.

. . .

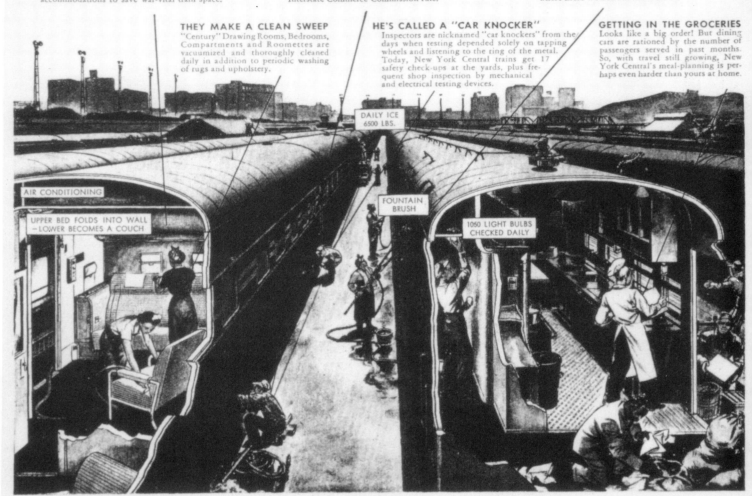

TRAVELING SURGERY
This operating room is mainly for dressings. But it is fully equipped. In an emergency, New York Central Representative would have train side-tracked, and the most delicate operation could be performed here.

THEY WEAR THE CADUCEUS
Enlisted men of the Medical Corps aid doctors and nurses. Their emblem, the staff and serpents of the Caduceus, is among the Army's proudest . . . with a tradition of brave and selfless service.

SHE RATES A SALUTE
The Army Nurse rates a salute . . . not only because she's a Lieutenant . . . but for her superb, often heroic service. The Army urgently needs 2,000 more trained nurse volunteers each month this year.

DIETS FROM KITCHEN CAR
Tasty, strengthening meals, prepared by Army cooks, are brought from the Hospital Kitchen Car. Men on special diets get trays first. When Ward Cars are attached to a regular New York Central train, the dining-car crew prepares and serves this invalid fare.

SCHOOL BOYS MADE THESE
Bath trays, designed by the Army Medical Department, hold basin, alcohol and powder. They are made in manual training by Junior Red Cross boys.

DOOR FOR LIFTING LITTERS IN OR OUT

OPERATING TABLE

TOP BUNK FORMS SEAT BACK

ASH TRAY & WATER GLASS

AN M.D. IS C.O.
Train Commander is a physician of the Army Medical Department, usually a Captain or Major. His orders control every person and every detail of life aboard this traveling hospital.

REPRESENTING THE RAILROAD
A New York Central Passenger Representative rides each Hospital Train. He acts for the railroad, aiding Train Commander with transportation, supplies and many other matters.

DITTY BAGS GO HERE
Patients keep personal possessions in "Ditty Bags" under bunks. Other luggage goes in baggage car, forward. Many New York Central baggage cars are on military duty. That's why *you* are asked to travel light.

"THANKS FOR THOSE BOOKS!"
Each Ward Car has a library of books donated by the public. More would be welcome, especially humor and mystery stories. New records, too, are needed for Ward Car phonographs.

UNITED STATES ARMY
MEDICAL DEPARTMENT
HOSPITAL WARD CAR

Your War Bonds help build Army Hospital Cars

Trains in White

How Army Hospital Trains speed wounded fighters homeward over the Water Level Route

MILE AFTER MILE, these travelers drink in each new picture framed in the windows of their Ward Dressing Car. It may be the scenic Hudson River, the rich fields of the Mohawk Valley, or the blazing furnaces of some war production center. But, always, it's *home* . . . "the good old U.S.A."

This is the last lap of the long, long journey through which the Army Medical Department has brought these wounded fighters. A journey that may have begun on a stretcher, under fire . . . but is ending now amid the care and comfort of a modern "hospital on wheels."

In this supreme service, New York Central is proud to share. Special schedules are timed to fit Medical Department needs. Speeds are planned for maximum comfort over every part of the route, and engineers exert all their skill in smooth train operation. For aboard these "trains in white" ride America's most honored passengers.

NEW YORK CENTRAL SYSTEM

New York Central
ONE OF AMERICA'S RAILROADS—ALL UNITED FOR VICTORY

NURSE'S DESK

BAGGAGE CAR WARD CAR WARD DRESSING CAR WARD CARS KITCHEN CAR WARD DRESSING CAR WARD CARS PERSONNEL CAR

"From the Ground Up"

America's pioneers started "from the ground up." Faced by trackless forests, mountains and deserts—beset by countless dangers—they accepted the challenge. Timbers were felled, broad acres cultivated, railroads built. All this was accomplished because our pioneers believed in the doctrine of individual enterprise; believed that hard labor, courage and faith would be rewarded.

Today, we're faced with another challenge. More food is required to supplement our nation's farm production. There's only one answer: "Victory Gardens"—thousands of them. *It's everybody's job* to produce food for our armed forces and home front workers . . . food for our own families. Again we're starting—from the ground up—to help hasten victory, to help maintain the spirit of individual enterprise in your America.

★ *Let's observe true Americanism. Avoid paying over-ceiling prices. Shun black markets . . . and buy bonds.*

THE PROGRESSIVE
UNION PACIFIC
RAILROAD

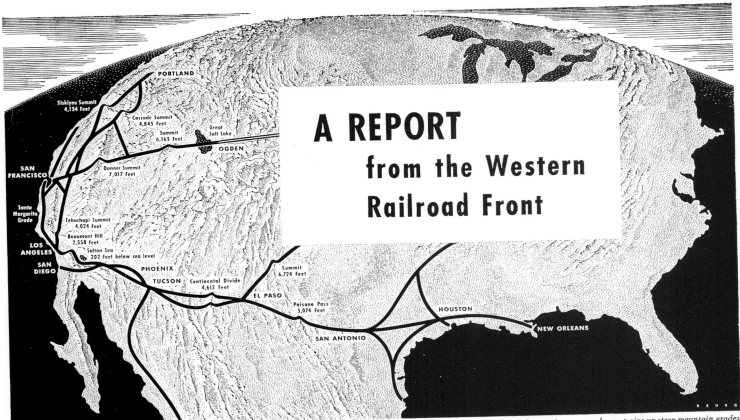

A REPORT from the Western Railroad Front

This map shows the major summits on Southern Pacific Lines. It takes more locomotives to move heavy trains up steep mountain grades.

Everywhere on this map the war trains are rolling.

All night long you can hear them whistling to each other in the lonely mountain passes. All day you can see them rumbling across the deserts.

From New Orleans in the deep South to San Francisco by the Golden Gate. From Ogden in Utah's gaunt Wasatch Mountains. From Portland in the evergreen Pacific Northwest, from Tucumcari, from San Antonio, from El Paso on the Rio Grande. Over Donner Summit, Cascade Summit and the Siskiyous. Through Paisano Pass and Carriso Gorge. Across the Sabine River, the Neches, the Pecos, the Colorado. Everywhere on Southern Pacific's 15,000 miles of line, the war trains are rolling.

Trainloads of men bound for "somewhere in the Pacific." Trainloads of tanks and guns. Trainloads of steel for the sprawling shipyards in the San Francisco, Los Angeles and Portland areas. Trainloads of engines and parts for the humming aircraft plants. Thousands of war trains rolling westward.

This is a report from Southern Pacific, the West's biggest railroad. Like all American railroads, we

need more men, more cars and locomotives to do the job. Like all American railroads, we are doing our best with what we have.

Look at the map. See how our lines converge on the Pacific Coast, the springboard for our offensive against Japan. Add to this the fact that we serve more military and naval establishments than any other railroad, and you can see how grave is our responsibility to our country. The war trains *must* come first.

Yet the other trains must roll, too. Long yellow "reefer" trains loaded with western fruits and vegetables important to the nation's health . . . 50,000 carloads of lettuce from California and Arizona . . .

60,000 cars of oranges and lemons and grapefruit from Southern California, Southern Arizona and the Rio Grande Valley down in Texas. Trainloads of lumber from Oregon and Washington for cantonments and emergency housing. Trainloads of salt from Louisiana, sulphur from Texas and potash from

Trona for explosives and chemicals. Trainloads of oil and gasoline from California and Texas. Copper from Arizona, Nevada and Utah. Cement. Sand. Gravel. Cattle. Sheep. Thousands of trains rolling east with the war trains insistently pouring west!

We are moving it all over a railroad that crosses more mountain ranges than any other in the country—with ten major summits, from the 2,500-foot hump at Beaumont Hill to the 7,000-foot Donner Pass, where the average annual snowfall is *thirty-six feet*, and great rotary plows whine through the drifts.

Our dispatchers are putting more trains over the line than they ever dreamed they could. And the old-timers don't talk about the "good old days" any more. They're *really* railroading now!

Many people did not believe we could carry the load we are carrying now. Our whole organization of 90,000 men and women is on its toes, thrilled to have an important part in the war effort and determined to keep 'em rolling.

A. T. MERCIER, *President*

"YOU BET THIS IS A MECHANIZED WAR"

HERE in the United States, mechanization rests upon more than 41,000 locomotives — more than 2,000,000 freight cars — speeding on their own highways of 230,000 miles of rail lines.

As the U. S. Army says in an official manual,

"Rail transportation provides a service which insures that a body of troops and their impedimenta will be transported to destination with the least amount of inconvenience and fatigue. The railroads can supply equipment so combined...as to accommodate passengers, freight, livestock, vehicles, ammunition, baggage, and practically all else tendered for transportation."

And more and more freight, these days, is being "tendered for transportation" by rail — and is being handled as tendered.

That is being done because of twenty years of planning and improvement since the last war, and because, since war started in Europe in 1939, the railroads have steadily increased their capacity to keep pace with the country's rising production.

How much more they can do depends upon the materials for repair and maintenance, and for additional cars and locomotives, which they are permitted to get. Whatever that may be, the railroads will continue to make the fullest use of all their resources in their vital part of this mechanized war.

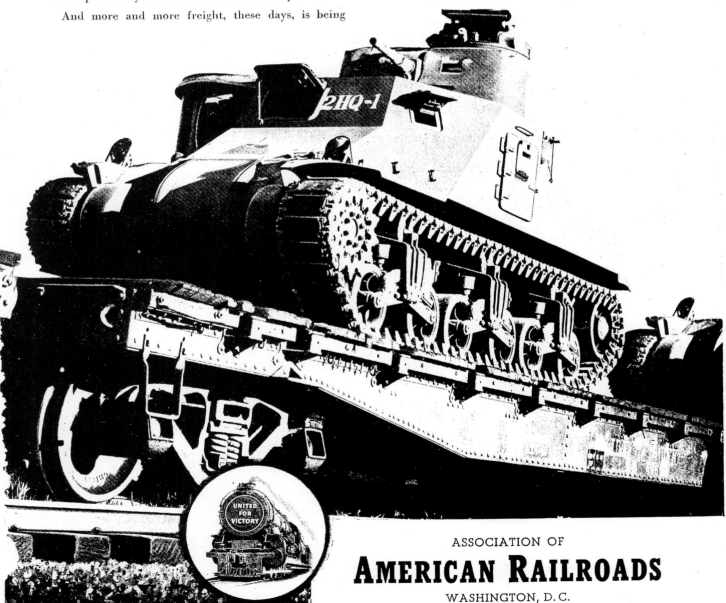

ASSOCIATION OF

AMERICAN RAILROADS
WASHINGTON, D.C.

N&W conductor signaling the engineer that all are aboard. N&W RY